Through WELSH BORDER COUNTRY

following OFFA'S DYKE PATH

Also by MARK RICHARDS
The COTSWOLD WAY
  (3rd impression)

NORTH CORNWALL
EXPLORING THE COASTAL PATH
  (2nd Edition)

Both published by
Thornhill Press Ltd.

THROUGH WELSH BORDER COUNTRY
following
Offa's Dyke Path

Plas Newydd at Llangollen

Mark Richards

Thornhill Press Ltd.

Published by
Thornhill Press Ltd.
46 Westgate Street,
Gloucester.

©Mark Richards 1976

ISBN: Hardback 0 904110 29 X
ISBN: Limp Cover 0 904110 53 2

Important note for readers of this book

Whilst every possible care has been taken to ensure the accuracy of the information contained within this Guide, neither the Author nor Publisher accept any liability regarding the information contained herein or its interpretation by readers. The Author invites observations and constructive criticism from readers for consideration in future editions.

Produced by
Oxford Publishing Co. Oxford

Printed by
B.H. Blackwell (Printing) Ltd.
in the City of Oxford

To Helen —
my beloved wife.

ACKNOWLEDGEMENTS

I wish to record my thanks to Ernie and Kathy Kay, Tony Drake and Frank Noble for their encouragement throughout the creation of this book, who along with Jack Baker and Arthur Roberts ensured that, as far as possible, the route of Offa's Dyke Path was accurately portrayed. I extend additional thanks to H. Noel Jerman, Chairman of Offa's Dyke Association, for kindly contributing the foreword.

My thanks and admiration go to Chris Jęsty, who produced the splendid panorama of Snowdonia from Moel Famau (page 20). Through his sensitive understanding of extensive views and meticulous recording, many more people are able to appreciate the details not only of this panorama but also of the view from Snowdon Summit. He has been working on other summits in North Wales together with Scafell Pike in the Lake District, thereby producing a permanent documentary record.

I wish to record my special thanks to Mr. A. Wainwright for all his encouragement and advice, which formed the foundation, and continues as an inspiration, of my work.

OFFA'S DYKE ASSOCIATION

The Offa's Dyke Association was formed prior to the opening of the long-distance footpath since when it has endeavoured to fulfil the following important roles:
- to promote harmonious relations between those who live and work along the course of the Path and visitors,
- to ensure that maintenance needs are met,
- to see that the needs of visitors for accommodation and for information are looked after,
- and to act as a forum for archaeological work.

As an example of its facilities I have, in writing this book, had access to a wide range of knowledge and advice which otherwise would not have been easy to obtain. For details of membership, publications, accommodation lists etc. write, with S.A.E. please, to Offa's Dyke Association (MR), West Street, Knighton, Powys.

CONTENTS

*cover illustrations — Offa's Dyke near Discoed
and Powis Castle*

Foreword

by

The Chairman of the Offa's Dyke Association

I am sure that I am expressing the wishes of all members of the Association in commending this new guide-book by Mark Richards, based on Offa's Dyke and the associated Long-Distance Footpath. It is the purpose of the Association to promote the conservation, improvement and better knowledge of the Welsh Border Region along the Dyke. We therefore warmly welcome anything that will contribute to the fuller understanding and appreciation by those who come to see the Dyke, to walk the Path, and to enjoy the lovely countryside through which they run.

This is a book with a difference, for instead of the maps and illustrations being a complement to the text, the text is rather a complement to the annotated maps and delightful illustrations. True, there is some introductory text providing background information; but it is the smaller-scale maps which will enable the reader to appreciate the setting of the Dyke and the Path in their borderland context, and it is the larger-scale maps and three hundred or so illustrations which will provide both the dedicated walkers and the more casual visitors—who will probably have come in their cars—with the detailed information they need to enhance their enjoyment of whatever part of our borderland, with its palimpsest of history, they have chosen to explore.

Particularly helpful for those visitors who are perhaps not-so-young will be the novel profile of the official line of the Path indicating where the route rises and falls and by how much, and indicating also the exact relationship of the Path to the Dyke itself. The guide will also be valuable in these days of rapid change in that the information it contains is not only selected for its relevance to the users of the Path and to visitors to the borderland but is up-to-date as well.

Mark Richards' guide-book will take a special place in the succession of books about the Welsh Border Country as bringing something new into the pattern of such books. Its handy size, its attractive lay-out and its informative content cannot but have a strong appeal—not just to those who are in search of knowledge for their visit to our border country but also to those who wish to take away with them something which, in after days, will evoke memories of their visit. What could be more evocative than the visual images which the excellent series of illustrations in the book so bountifully provide?

All of us in the Association are grateful to Mark Richards for his interest and his help in the task which we have set ourselves. We wish his new venture every success.

April 1976

H. Noel Jerman

Offa's Dyke above Churchtown

Introduction

Trwy'r Gororau ar hyd llwybr Clawdd Offa

A Frontier March

Offa's Dyke Path is a long-distance footpath created by the Countryside Commission, running for the main part in Wales 'from sea to sea' between Prestatyn in the north and Sedbury Cliffs near Chepstow in the south, for a total distance of 274½km (173 miles). The route is based upon the ancient frontier earthwork between Celtic Cymru and Saxon Mercia, but is by no means exclusively restricted to its company. For in two distinct areas the Path is well away from Offa's Dyke, taking the opportunity of enjoying in the south the unrestricted walking available over the Black Mountains and in the north the Clwydian Range of hills, which together greatly enhance the scenic quality of the route. Along the way are Iron Age hill-forts and great Norman castles, ancient churches and old market towns, lovely hills and green meadows, popular holiday centres and little-frequented communities tucked away among the rolling hills of this border region, and, of course, Offa's Dyke, which soon becomes something of an old friend.

This book is a personal record of two years exploration of this fascinating pathway, during which time it became clear to me that what was required was a sure reference to the exact course of Offa's Dyke Path, thereby affording walkers the freedom to go as far as they wished without the risk of straying. My own interest in pen drawing has allowed me to illustrate features and scenes that I felt would be relevant and of interest to fellow walkers, and I hope that readers will derive an increased pleasure from their own forays both on foot or by car along the route of Offa's Dyke Path. I will not attempt to discuss the details of the Path and its numerous rewarding alternatives here in the introduction, the main body of the book achieves this adequately, yet I feel it is important to provide some background to the Path and in particular to Offa's Dyke.

The creation of a footpath route

The modern border between England and Wales runs an erratic course through the Marches, contrasting with the positive line of Offa's Dyke, a bold north/south frontier wavering little. The original Mercian architect, King Offa, was not deterred by the difficulties of topography, in fact he used the ley of the land so expertly that one cannot but marvel at the enterprise and skill he employed.

Offa's Dyke Path is unique among the long-distance routes so far designated, for it has adopted this archaeological feature as its theme. Coupled with the variety and intricate beauty of the Welsh Border Country it was not surprising that the National Parks Commission (later Countryside Commission) made early plans to create an 'historic route from sea to sea'. Unfortunately, the project was slow to gain momentum from the time of its designation in 1955 to its eventual opening, despite much general interest. However, an official opening was fixed for 10th July, 1971 and negotiations were concluded to create the necessary new rights-of-way and erect stiles and footbridges, together with all the important waymarking. The Offa's Dyke Association, a dedicated group of people concerned for the Welsh Borderland and in particular the proposed footpath route along Offa's Dyke, was an important factor and prime moving influence in the run up to this opening.

An appropriate and central place was found for the opening ceremony at Knighton, a market town in the heart of Clun Forest, whose old Welsh name Tref-y-clawdd (Town on the Dyke) relates directly to its situation on Offa's Dyke. The purchasing of a particularly vulnerable section of Offa's Dyke in the town and the land immediately around it by the Tref-y-clawdd 1970 Society as their contribution to European Conservation Year, provided a focal point for these celebrations. This, the Offa's Dyke Riverside Park, was opened by Lady Green Price, President of the Society, and was followed by the formal opening of Offa's Dyke long-distance footpath by Lord Hunt (Sir John Hunt of Everest fame).

What and where is Offa's Dyke?

The first major and comprehensive study of Offa's Dyke carried out by Sir Cyril Fox in the 1920's and 30's opened a new interest in this earthwork, which even today retains a good many of its secrets, despite more recent site investigation. Offa's Dyke belongs to a period in our history commonly known as the 'Dark Ages', that span of centuries between the departure of the Romans and the arrival of the Normans, so called because little documentary evidence has survived of those times, upon which certain theories could be based. However, all available evidence suggests that Offa, King of the Saxon kingdom of Mercia (757–796 A.D.) can be credited with having created the necessary unified strength within his expanding domain and commanding sufficient respect to initiate the construction of the great Dyke. He is said to have led his forces in a series of battles with the Celtic Britons of Cymru and it is likely that during a period of comparative peace he negotiated with the Welsh Princes a boundary bank to run the length of the border to protect Saxon settlement from the guerilla tactics of the hillmen. It is thought that the main trade routes along the dry ridgeways, where today we often see slightly larger banks, were first to be built and that the rest of the construction was completed within a comparatively short time.

Archaeologists differ quite widely in their opinions as to the extent, alignment and detailed purpose of the construction, for in the north the Dyke peters out unexplainedly at Treuddyn north of Wrexham. There is the added complication of Wat's Dyke, a very similar earthwork, presumed to be of a somewhat earlier date, but nothing is known of 'Wat'. Maybe the two Dykes were associated, with Offa's Dyke an expression of renewed strength, forcing a modified line a little further west of previous Saxon settlement—or was it that Wat's Dyke was the later boundary mark, a reflection of retreat?

In the south the Dyke, having run a strong course down through the central Marches, breaks up into short lengths across the Herefordshire Plain from Rushock Hill, reaching the River Wye at Bridge Sollers near Hereford. The River Wye itself must have been considered a satisfactory frontier line for apart from a brief return above Welsh Bicknor it does not appear again until, rather surprisingly, it is found running along the plateau edge high above the river on Highbury Plain, a short way south of Monmouth. This alignment is particularly interesting because the Wye has forged an obvious natural barrier. The probable explanation for this seemingly pointless effort could be that, if we accept that the boundary was a mutual compromise of interest, the Welsh would have required complete freedom of passage up and down what was for them a main trading river, with both banks available for landing. Nevertheless, the Mercians wished to impress their self-confidence upon their opponents by building an imposing bulwark where it could be seen and appreciated. The southern limit of the Dyke was, in contrast with the north, most definite; the Beachley peninsula was left to the Welsh by constructing the earthwork across the neck of high ground from the limestone cliffs above the Wye to Sedbury Cliffs overlooking the broadening River Severn, thus completing a frontier line, which early chronicles claimed ran 'from sea to sea' but this is hard to substantiate on the visual evidence that remains today.

It is perhaps ironical that although the Dyke has largely withstood the ravages of time and man, it probably only lasted as a meaningful border for a mere forty years. Yet this simple earthen bank today symbolizes one thousand years of Anglo-Celtic relations, unlike its earlier and more striking Roman counterpart, Hadrian's Wall, which reflects little of Anglo-Scottish history. Along and around its course the great waves of history have flowed and because this is an area of fusion and flux only rarely does Offa's Dyke still enjoy the role of dividing line. Offa's Dyke Path, on the other hand, has come to express a unification of the men of the hills with the men of the plains, not a division.

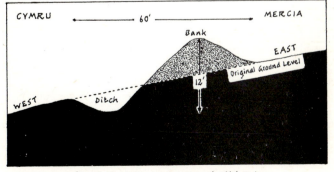

A profile of the basic construction of Offa's Dyke

This profile of Offa's Dyke's construction can, of course, only give a general impression of the earthwork, remembering that it is likely that numerous gangs, recruited from a wide area of western Mercian settlement, would have been employed to accomplish the entire enterprise, each working within their own experience to their own slightly different patterns. Naturally the problems of topography would have greatly influenced how they could or could not tackle the job. For instance, on flat or slightly westward sloping ground (as in the profile on p.XI), the boundary bank would have been thrown up leaving a deep trench on the Welsh side. Steeper ground required a ditch to be dug on both sides in order that enough earth was available; when it came to excessively steep slopes often there would not have been a ditch at all or at most a slight shelf-effect created. On a few occasions the ditch appears solely on the eastern flank, which could simply reflect a misunderstanding between the overall architect and the particular gangs engaged on those sections.

Erosion threats

Over the years the Dyke has fallen victim to a great many inroads and erosion both natural and man-made has much depleted this one-time mighty earthwork. Agriculture would seem to have been a principal adversary; often as one wanders along the long-distance footpath one is amazed by the way the bank and ditch can appear and disappear within a little distance, the result of encroachment by the plough. The Dyke had a number of original 'Yatts' or gates, but over the years many new gaps have breached the bank to meet the changing needs of farmers and road builders. Streams have cut deep courses in the ditch and, where the Dyke was constructed across river meadows, flooding has swept it away without trace.

The creation of a long-distance footpath following Offa's Dyke is in itself a small yet significant erosion threat, and it behoves walkers to consider the future of the Dyke as a visible Dark Age monument and treat it with respect. The development of a path along the crest of the bank is a state of affairs that might well suit landowners (who for their part consider the least interference with agricultural practice to be of paramount importance) but this is adversely affecting the vulnerable Dyke, which cannot be re-created, only re-constructed.

Walking the Path

Walking for most people is a familiar and necessary activity, yet for some reason those who walk for pleasure are and will no doubt always be in a minority, which is perhaps fortunate; for theirs is the intimate experience of exploring the countryside away from petrol fumes and the immediacy of time. Offa's Dyke Path holds a special appeal, for the very nature of it induces a slow pace, it is no way for the speed merchant either in his car or on foot; the roads are often narrow and the Path through this prime stock-rearing country, home of Hereford cattle and Clun Forest sheep, works a way through an intricate network of fieldpaths and byways. It may have been more appropriate to call the walk the 'Welsh Marches Path' which would have clarified to some extent what the route is all about. However, Offa's Dyke Path has the stronger appeal, so it is worth giving a few figures to illustrate that this is in fact more than just a walk along a forgotten frontier. Offa's Dyke Path is 274½km long whilst the original Mercian border extended to only 240km, of which distance only 128km of actual earthwork were ever constructed, the Path and Dyke being co-incident for a mere 107km which represent three-quarters of its length and includes the best preserved sections of the remaining earthen bank and ditch.

Having walked numerous stretches of the Path before embarking on the mapping for this guide, I was satisfied that it was generally preferable to walk southward from Prestatyn, completing the journey impressively with Offa's Dyke overlooking the Severn estuary upon Sedbury Cliffs. Putting aside the psychological factors which must colour each individual's choice, I live in the south, hence it would be only natural for me to, as it were, head homeward. This north/south policy enabled me to present a natural sequence of the strip-maps through the book—there is nothing more frustrating than to get lost in your guidebook before setting a foot on the actual Path! It has been found that the majority of Dyke Path wayfarers in fact choose to walk northward, which has its merits, no doubt; the layout of this book, however, should make it possible for anyone to walk in whichever direction they choose with almost equal facility.

Route finding

It is appropriate to explain the different forms of waymarking instigated by the Countryside Commission, who together with the local District Councils are responsible for the erection and maintenance of stiles, footbridges and waymarking along the route. They fall into two main categories, (a) a tall oak signpost is largely employed, at points where the Path either leaves a motor road or changes direction, on which the English 'OFFA'S DYKE PATH' or Welsh 'LLWYBR CLAWDD OFFA' or sometimes bi-lingual lettering is used. There is also a low concrete plinth cast with the same choice of lettering. (b) the acorn symbol, used on all official long-distance routes either in simple stencil form or on a metal plate, sited where the walker may be in doubt, thereby restoring confidence to march resolutely on.

Be prepared!

Regular walkers respect their hobby and equip themselves appropriately in comfortable clothing; they may walk optimistically but they bear in mind from experience that the weather can be a fickle thing and always carry wind and waterproof anoraks or at least a light-weight cagoule. Proper footwear, boots or strong shoes with woollen socks are important to a walker, in fact attention to these basic details are crucial to the full enjoyment of walking even when only comparatively short distances are being considered. By the very nature of the way I record my walks, fieldwork is done covering short stretches at a time; nevertheless, it is better to be safe than sorry and I pack together with my anorak, a sweater, balaclava and gloves, food (as an energy reserve—a bar of chocolate or raisins are excellent), a drink (hot or cold dependent on season of year), a simple first-aid kit, an emergency blanket (Space brand by Thermos), whistle, torch and some money all tucked inside a plastic bag within a nylon rucksack.

When to walk

Most people will be encouraged in the spring and early summer to go out into the countryside and maybe take the opportunity of discovering Offa's Dyke Path for themselves. This is the best season to come for settled weather, and the Path is less likely to be impeded by the wandering tendrils of thorns and nettles, which discourage the wearing of shorts and skirts. Intense sun, high winds, driving rain, dense mist or deep snow all detract from the pleasures of walking; nevertheless, any time in the year good conditions can prevail, indeed my fondest memories of the Path are of winter expeditions when all was calm and serene, and of a romantic moonlight stroll along the banks of the River Wye between Bigsweir and Brockweir one Christmas Eve.

Useful Ordnance Survey maps

For anyone considering exploratory visits into the Welsh Border Country there is one thing I would recommend above all else (even before this book!) and that is the Ordnance Survey Quarter-Inch map of Wales and the Marches, which is the most practical source of information for general planning, giving a clear attractive view of all the country traversed by Offa's Dyke Path. The 1:50,000 maps recently published by the Ordnance Survey provide the detail that makes it possible to drive, park and walk with a greater assurance. The specific sheets relevant to the Path are:

116 Denbigh and Colwyn Bay
117 Chester
126 Shrewsbury
137 Ludlow and Wenlock Edge
148 Presteigne and Hay-on-Wye
161 Abergavenny and The Black Mountains
162 Gloucester and Forest of Dean

They are, in contrast with the special Quarter-Inch sheet, somewhat expensive, which, hopefully, is where this book will be found to be of value.

Respect the Country Code

As a countryman, indeed a farmer, I feel it is important to conclude this introduction with a reference to the Country Code and its importance in the rural scene. The Countryside Commission have entered upon their task of reconciling two apparently conflicting interests i.e. landowners' and visitors', by presenting a code of conduct based upon good manners and respect of the vulnerable rural environment. The pressures on the countryside are great: for many it is a last haven to which they may retreat from the intensity of town and city life. For industry and commerce it is seen as a valuable resource to exploit. But for agriculturalists, it is not merely a means of livelihood, but resulting from the pressures of demand, as food is required in ever increasing quantities, so more is demanded of the same land. It is to this background that the Countryside Commission have presented their Code. Without countryside there is no retreat, without land there is no food, therefore it represents a future for us all. The Code is particularly relevant to this border walk with its constant passage between pastures and cultivated land. Further, the modern trend of reaching the start of a walk in a car calls for special consideration when parking that car. The large-scale maps within this book indicate the vicinity of possible parking spaces; but to be fair, it is up to each individual to choose a spot that neither blocks a gateway nor obstructs the view of traffic along the highway—it's no use quoting this book as authority to park.

The Country Code:

1 Guard against all risk of fire
2 Fasten all gates, unless they are obviously intended to be left open
3 Keep dogs under proper control
4 Keep to paths across farmland
5 Avoid damaging fences, hedges and walls
6 Do not leave litter
7 Safeguard water supplies
8 Protect wild life, plants and trees
9 Go carefully on country roads
10 Respect the life of the countryside

OFFA'S DYKE PATH

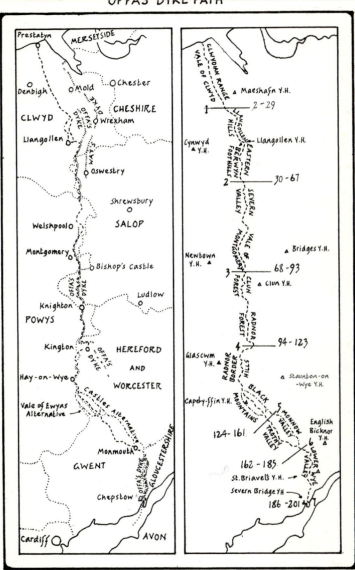

SYMBOLS & ABBREVIATIONS
USED IN LARGE SCALE MAPS

Map Scale 3" = 1 mile   North is top of every page

Route on motor road ⌒   Route on footpath - - - - -

Alternative routes and other footpaths ·-·-·-·-·-·-·

Offa's Dyke or other ancient earthworks

Hedge ⌒⌒⌒   Fence ++++++   Wall ∞∞∞∞∞∞

Contours (at 100' intervals)

700
800
900
1000   Crag

Trees : Conifers   Deciduous   Marshy ground

Stream ⌒   River ⇒ (arrows indicate the direction of flow)

Footbridge ⌒   Road bridge

Waterfall ⌒   Lake

Buildings ▪▪   Church or Chapel ▪▪ +

Unenclosed road =========   Railway

Ordnance Survey column △   Prominent cairns ▲

_11_ : Map continuation page number

⑬ : Kilometres from Prestatyn - on main route only

——— All other distances shown in miles

Abbreviations : O.S. = Ordnance Survey

Y.H. = Youth Hostel   P = Parking for at least one car - suggested

HALF-INCH MAP SYMBOLS

⊙ = Town or village with Post Office   O = Other communites

A.40 Major road with road number   Ⓣ = Telephone

Other motorable roads   .... Offa's Dyke

- - - - - Offa's Dyke Path   ·-·-·-· Alternative route

·-·-·- National boundary   (E.C.D.) = Early Closing Day

ILLUSTRATED GUIDE TO
OFFA'S DYKE PATH

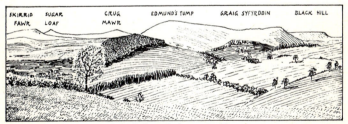

Westward from Pembridge Castle

The strip maps in this guide are based upon the ordnance survey 1:25000 (2½"), 1st series; with the sanction of the Controller of Her Majesty's Stationery Office. Crown copyright reserved.

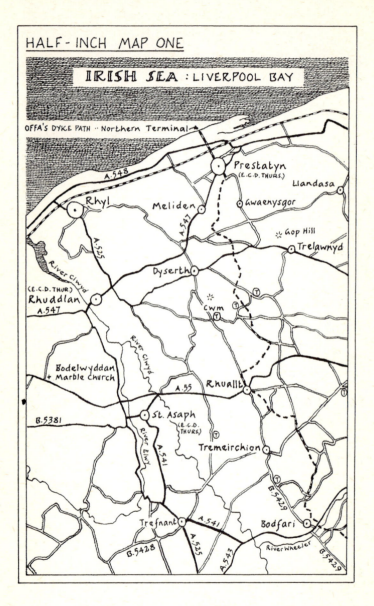

IRISH SEA : LIVERPOOL BAY

OFFA's DYKE PATH ·· Northern Terminal →

A.548

Prestatyn
(E.C.D. THURS.)

Llandasa

Rhyl

Meliden

Gwaenysgor

A.541

Gop Hill

Trelawnyd

A.525

Dyserth

River Clwyd

(E.C.D. THUR)
Rhuddlan
A.547

Cwm

River Clwyd

Bodelwyddan
+ Marble Church

A.55

Rhuallt

B.5381

St. Asaph
(E.C.D. THURS.)

River Elwy

Tremeirchion

A.541

B.5429

Trefnant

A.541

Bodfari

B.5428

A.525

A.543

River Wheeler

B.5429

2

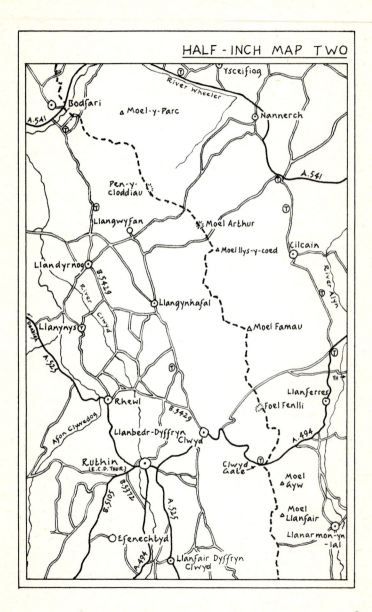

3

Prestatyn railway station

(right)
Gop Hill from the south.
The tumulus surmounting
this prominent hill
(limestone) is thought
to be a bronze age
burial cairn, though
little has been found
during excavations,
giving strength to the
theory that it was a
maritime beacon
after the stamp of
St. Elmo's Summer House.

(below)
The quarried
northern slopes
of Moel Hiraddog

PRESTATYN TO FISH MOUNTAIN

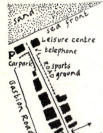

Westward from the front at Prestatyn.

Although Prestatyn has become a modern recreational centre very much of our time, it should not be assumed to be a place without its share of history. For not only has there been a small Norman castle within its bounds, but a Roman fort and contempary artifacts were uncovered a short distance from the parish church. Furthermore a chipping floor, probably for the production of flint tools, was found providing evidence of some form of occupation stretching back several thousand years.

PRESTATYN

The name derives from priest's ton, a monastic community.

The first Offa's Dyke Path way-mark is to be found at the top of the High Street.

Ffordd : road
las : green

The path, that ascends from the steep minor road to Gwaenysgor, affords splendid views over Prestatyn and beyond, to the other popular coastal resorts of Rhyl, Abergele and Colwyn Bay. The distant twin limestone headlands of Little and Great Ormes further attract the westward gaze. Reminiscent of a cliff path, the route courts the rim of limestone quarries beneath ones feet, so take care — particularly on a day of fresh sea breezes!

Gop Hill and Gwaenysgor come into view at this point

There is a marvellous feeling of depth and breadth to the scene as one strides along the edge of this escarpment.

Certainly, walking south is to be preferred in these initial stages.

Ffordd-las, a quiet suburban road, leads to Bishopwood Road (marked 'A' on map), turning right then shortly left up a minor road continue round the first hairpin bend, ignoring a track to the right, and ascend to join a rising path by a wall leading off right.

9

5

Gwaenysgor Church

Rhuddlan Castle

Dyserth Falls - a very pretty sight but a little too accessible for full enjoyment, they are situated a mile to the west of the Path in private gardens (5p entry fee).

Marian Mill

Cwm Church and Inn

BLUE LION
INN

8

FISH MOUNTAIN TO TYDDYN-Y-CYLL

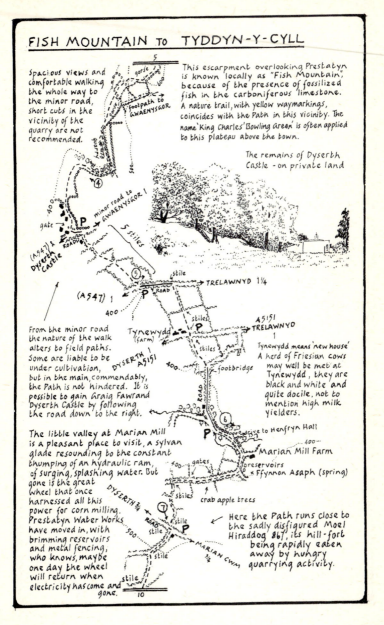

Spacious views and comfortable walking the whole way to the minor road, short cuts in the vicinity of the quarry are not recommended.

This escarpment overlooking Prestatyn is known locally as "Fish Mountain", because of the presence of fossilized fish in the carboniferous limestone. A nature trail, with yellow waymarkings, coincides with the Path in this vicinity. The name 'King Charles' Bowling Green' is often applied to this plateau above the town.

The remains of Dyserth Castle - on private land

TRELAWNYD 1¼

From the minor road the nature of the walk alters to field paths. Some are liable to be under cultivation, but in the main, commendably, the Path is not hindered. It is possible to gain Graig Fawr and Dyserth Castle by following the road down to the right.

Tynewydd means 'new house'. A herd of Friesian cows may well be met at Tynewydd, they are black and white and quite docile, not to mention high milk yielders.

The little valley at Marian Mill is a pleasant place to visit, a sylvan glade resounding to the constant thumping of an hydraulic ram, of surging, splashing water. But gone is the great wheel that once harnessed all this power for corn milling. Prestatyn Water Works have moved in, with brimming reservoirs and metal fencing, who knows, maybe one day the wheel will return when electricity has come and gone.

Here the Path runs close to the sadly disfigured Moel Hiraddog 867, its hill-fort being rapidly eaten away by hungry quarrying activity.

9

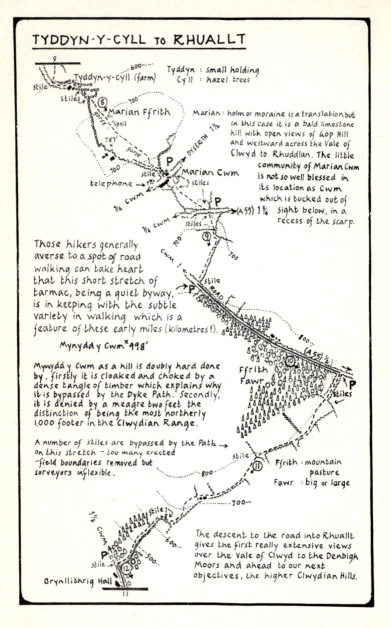

TYDDYN-Y-CYLL to RHUALLT

Tyddyn : small holding
Cyll : hazel trees

Tyddyn-y-cyll (farm)
stile
stiles
⑧
Marian Ffrith
spoil
787 ×
700
stile
telephone → cwm
¾ cwm

Marian : holm or moraine is a translation, but in this case it is a bald limestone hill with open views of Gop Hill and westward across the Vale of Clwyd to Rhuddlan. The little community of Marian Cwm is not so well blessed in its location as Cwm which is tucked out of sight below, in a recess of the scarp.

DYSERTH 1½
P
Marian Cwm
3 stiles
P
(A55) 1¼
stiles
⑨
cwm 1
700

Those hikers generally averse to a spot of road walking can take heart that this short stretch of tarmac, being a quiet byway, is in keeping with the subtle variety in walking which is a feature of these early miles (kilometres!).

P stile
ROAD
800
(A55) ½

Mynydd y Cwm × 998'

Mynydd y Cwm as a hill is doubly hard done by, firstly it is cloaked and choked by a dense tangle of timber which explains why it is bypassed by the Dyke Path. Secondly, it is denied by a meagre two feet the distinction of being the most northerly 1,000 footer in the Clwydian Range.

Ffrith Fawr
⑩
P
stiles

A number of stiles are bypassed by the Path → on this stretch – too many erected – field boundaries removed but surveyors inflexible.

stile
⑪
800

Ffrith : mountain pasture
Fawr : big or large

1½ cwm
stile
700
600
P
stile
⑫
500
Brynllibrig Hall

The descent to the road into Rhuallt gives the first really extensive views over the Vale of Clwyd to the Denbigh Moors and ahead to our next objectives, the higher Clwydian Hills.

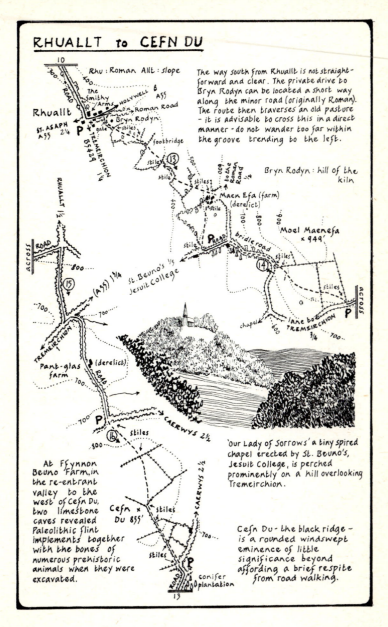

RHUALLT to CEFN DU

Rhu: Roman Allt: slope

The way south from Rhuallt is not straight-forward and clear. The private drive to Bryn Rodyn can be located a short way along the minor road (originally Roman). The route then traverses an old pasture – it is advisable to cross this in a direct manner – do not wander too far within the groove trending to the left.

Rhuallt

St. ASAPH A55 2¼

The Smithy Arms

HOLYWELL A55

Roman Road

Bryn Rodyn

gate   stiles

TREMEIRCHION B5429 1¼

footbridge

stiles **13**

stiles

Bryn Rodyn: hill of the kiln

Maen Efa (farm) (derelict)

stile

to the Roman Road

Moel Maenefa ×949'

RHUALLT 1½

ACROSS ROAD

stiles ROAD

bridle road

14

stiles

ACROSS

P

15

(A55) 1¾

St. Beuno's ⅕ Jesuit College

chapel

lane to TREMEIRCHION ¾

TREMEIRCHION

Pant-glas farm (derelict)

ROAD

P

CAERWYS 2½

'Our Lady of Sorrows' a tiny spired chapel erected by St. Beuno's, Jesuit College, is perched prominently on a hill overlooking Tremeirchion.

At Ffynnon Beuno Farm, in the re-entrant valley to the west of Cefn Du, two limestone caves revealed Paleolithic flint implements together with the bones of numerous prehistoric animals when they were excavated.

P **16** stiles

Cefn × Du 855'

stiles

CAERWYS 2½

stiles

Cefn Du – the black ridge – is a rounded windswept eminence of little significance beyond affording a brief respite from road walking.

ROAD

P

conifer plantation

13

The C3th tower and attractive black and white lychgate of Bodfari Church stand proudly on the hillside overlooking the Vale of Clwyd adjacent to the Dinorben Arms.

The River Wheeler (from the Welsh 'chwiler' = twisting) is, in truth, little more than a strong stream. The hill, rising beyond in this view is Moel-y-Parc.

CEFN DU to BODFARI

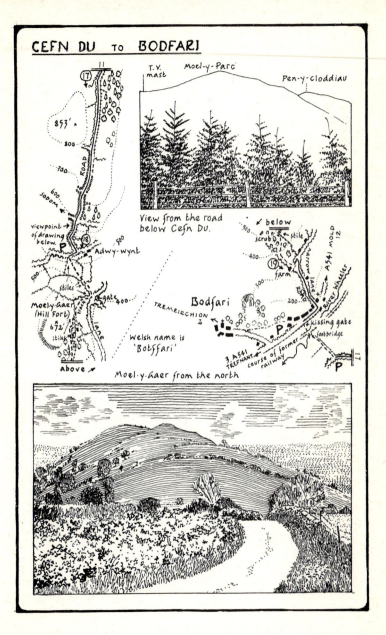

11

17

853'

800

700

600

500m

ROAD

viewpoint →
of drawing
below.

18

Adwy-wynt

500

stiles

gate 400

Moel·y·Gaer
(Hill Fort)

672'

stiles

above ↗

T.V.
mast

Moel-y-Parc

Pen-y-cloddiau

View from the road
below Cefn Du.

↙ below

scrub

stile

400

19

farm

A541 MOLD 12

300

ROAD

200

River Wheeler

↓ below

Bodfari

TREMEIRCHION
2

Welsh name is
'Botffari'

kissing gate

P

footbridge

3 A541
TREFNANT

course of former
railway

P

17

Moel·y·Gaer from the north

13

— St. Asaph Cathedral
A Cathedral site since 560 A.D.
The present structure was
completed in 1381 A.D. the
building having much to
commend it both in style
and dignity.

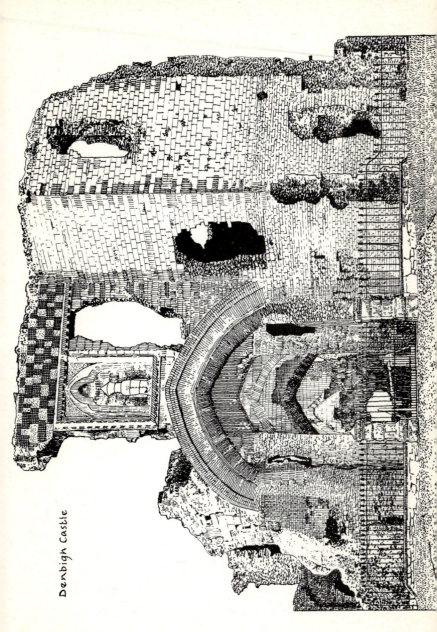

Denbigh Castle

15

Bodfari and Moel-y-Gaer (Iron Age hill-fort) from the Path above Grove Hall.

Penycloddiau from the track to Aifft

The Dyke Path follows the western ramparts of Pen-y-cloddiau hill-fort.

BODFARI TO PENYCLODDIAU

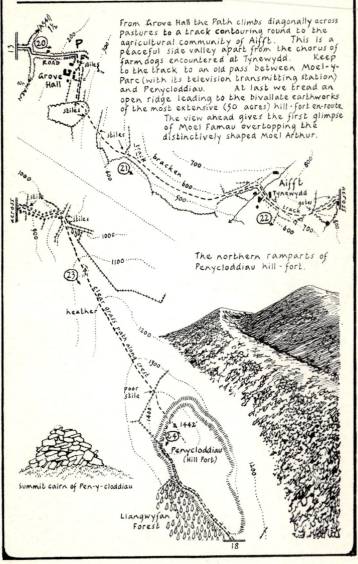

From Grove Hall the Path climbs diagonally across pastures to a track contouring round to the agricultural community of Aifft. This is a peaceful side valley apart from the chorus of farm dogs encountered at Tynewydd. Keep to the track to an old pass between Moel-y-Parc (with its television transmitting station) and Penycloddiau. At last we tread an open ridge leading to the bivallate earthworks of the most extensive (50 acres) hill-fort en-route.

The view ahead gives the first glimpse of Moel Famau overtopping the distinctively shaped Moel Arthur.

20

1½

13

200

P

ROAD

stiles

Grove Hall

stiles

stiles

track

bracken

21

400

500

600

700

Aifft

Tynewydd

gates

track

22

600

700

800

across

stile

across

900

1000

stiles

1000

1100

23

clear grass path along crest

heather

1200

1300

The northern ramparts of Penycloddiau hill-fort.

poor stile

1400

1442

24

Penycloddiau
(Hill Fort)

1200

1300

Summit cairn of Pen-y-cloddiau

Llangwyfan Forest

18

17

PENYCLODDIAU TO MOEL LLYS-Y-COED

17

25

stile

1100 1000 NANNERCH 2½

P

gate car park

stile

Llangwyfan Forest

LLANDYRNOG 2½

26

Moel Arthur presents quite a fierce obstacle to the long distance walker, even those hardened by the many ups and downs of border hills will do well to treat this ascent with respect. Few are they that romp over Moel Arthur with a heavy pack!

Phew!

The neatly proportioned summit of Moel Arthur is an obvious challenge for anyone wishing to claim a hill but with limited time to spare. Archaeological excavation on this hill top has yielded early Bronze Age axe heads, together with coarse Roman pottery.

1100

stile by boulder spoil 1200

1300

1400

1494 Moel Arthur (Hill Fort)

Moel Arthur is a special 'Country Park', owned by the Clwyd County Council.

If you pass this way during holiday times or weekends a diverse mixture of humanity can be encountered enjoying the space and freedom of these hills in their various fashions.

27

cattle grid P stile

(A541) 2¼ car park

1100 LLANDYRNOG ¾

1100

Descending southward from Moel Arthur be wary of the two open quarries that scar this slope, although it is harder to stay on one's feet it is certainly safer to keep close to the wall.

1200

1300

1400

Moel Llys-y-Coed

28

Moel-y-Parc and Moel Arthur from Moel Llys-y-coed.

19

MOEL LLYS-Y-COED TO MOEL DYWYLL

Moel Famau   Foel Fenlli   Moel Dywyll

from Moel Llys-y-Coed

The pretty double
-aisled Cilcain
Church, standing
in an oval church-
yard shaded by
sycamore trees.

1400

1300

1300

1400

29

track to CILCAIN 2

1½ LLANGYNHAFAL

Moel
Dywyll

A delightful moorland
ridge walk on a clear
pedestrian highway.

30
1½
21

18

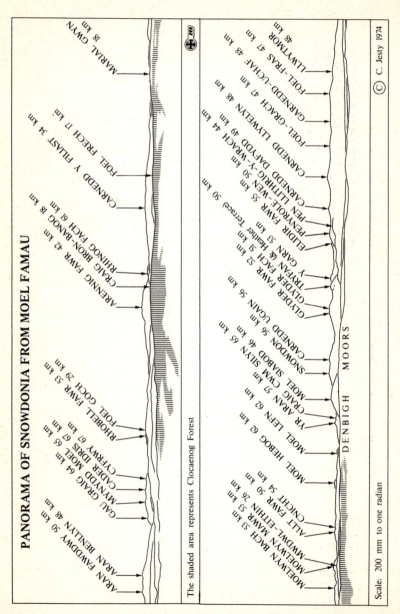

PANORAMA OF SNOWDONIA FROM MOEL FAMAU

The shaded area represents Clocaenog Forest

Scale: 200 mm to one radian

© C. Jesty 1974

DENBIGH MOORS

MARIAL GWYN 18 km

FOEL FRECH 17 km
CAERNEDD Y FILIAST 34 km

RHINOG FACH 61 km
CRAIG BRON-BANOG 18 km
ARENNIG FAWR 42 km

FOEL GOCH 29 km
RHOBELL FAWR 53 km
CADER IDRIS 67 km
CYFRWY 67 km
MOEL MYNYDD 65 km
GAU GRAIG 64 km

ARAN BENLLYN 50 km
ARAN FAWDDWY 50 km

LLWYTMOR 48 km
FOEL-FRAS 47 km
GARNEDD-UCHAF 47 km
CARNEDD LLYWELYN 48 km
FOEL-GRACH 47 km
PEN LLITHRIG-Y-WRACH 44 km
CARNEDD DAFYDD 49 km
PENYROLE-WEN 50 km
ELIDIR FAWR 55 km
Y GARN 53 km
TRYFAN 51 km
GLYDER FACH 51 km
GLYDER FAWR 52 km
CARNEDD UGAIN 56 km
SNOWDON 56 km
MOEL SIABOD 46 km
CWM SILYN 65 km
CRAIG CWM SILYN 57 km
ARAN 57 km
YR ARAN 62 km
MOEL LEFN 62 km
MOEL HEBOG 62 km

CNICHT 54 km
ALLT FAWR 50 km
MWDWL-EITHIN 26 km
MOELWYN MAWR 53 km
MOELWYN BACH 53 km

The shaded area represents Clocaenog Forest

MOEL DYWYLL TO MOEL FAMAU

European Conservation Year 1970 was the inspiration for many a good deed, one such was the tremendous effort mounted upon the greatly dilapidated Tower crowning the utmost summit of the Clwydian Range, Moel Famau. The structure was built in the year 1810 to commemorate fifty years of King George III's reign. Designed by Thomas Harrison as a two-tiered obelisk with the lower portions reminiscent of some Egyptian tomb, it collapsed in 1862 since when it has stood forlorn against the ravages of time, a crumbling ruin.

Dyke Path walkers attain this prize summit from the north following a seemingly endless trudge along the undulating ridge from Moel Llys-y-coed. However, monotony is relieved by virtue of the view westward, where, as the diagram opposite indicates, the whole sweep of the Snowdonian Mountains beyond the Denbigh Moors are an uplifting sight for those walkers with hills in their hearts.

Viewpoint par excellence

This recent enterprise, though somewhat belated, has given new life to what otherwise would have been but a decaying heap of rubble.

For now, more than ever, weekend trippers take to their feet and ascending the broad track from Bwlch Pen Barras claim for themselves this exciting viewpoint. A view indicator set into the inner walls must add greatly to the enjoyment of many visitors blessed with clear visibility.

Map labels: 19 · 1500 · Pwll-y-rhos · 1500 · 1600 · 1700 · 1400 · 31 · burnt heather · Offa's Path · Moel Famau 1820' · O.S. column number 2961 · 32 · 1500 · 1500 · 1500 · Part of the plantations of Clwyd Forest · 23

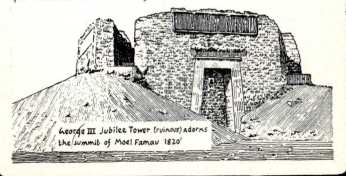

George III Jubilee Tower (ruinous) adorns the summit of Moel Famau 1820'

21

Two views of Moel Famau "the mother mountain" from the east.
① The newly afforested (Clwyd Forest) slopes above The Loggerheads.
② The ruinous summit tower as seen from Cilcain

22

MOEL FAMAU TO FOEL FENLLI

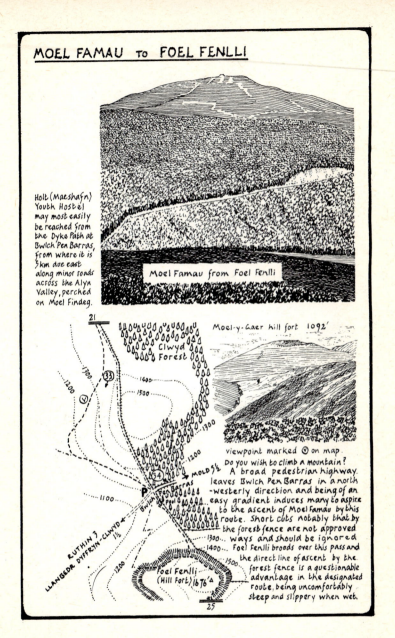

Moel Famau from Foel Fenlli

Holt (Maeshafn) Youth Hostel may most easily be reached from the Dyke Path at Bwlch Pen Barras, from where it is 5km due east along minor roads across the Alyn Valley, perched on Moel Findeg.

Moel-y-Gaer hill fort 1092'

Clwyd Forest

viewpoint marked ⊙ on map.

Do you wish to climb a mountain? A broad pedestrian highway leaves Bwlch Pen Barras in a north-westerly direction and being of an easy gradient induces many to aspire to the ascent of Moel Famau by this route. Short cuts notably that by the forest fence are not approved ways and should be ignored. Foel Fenlli broods over this pass and the direct line of ascent by the forest fence is a questionable advantage in the designated route, being uncomfortably steep and slippery when wet.

MOLD 5½

RUTHIN 3

LLANGEDR DYFFRYN-CLWYD

Foel Fenlli (Hill Fort) 1676'

The great ramparts of Foel Fenlli hill-fort from the north.

Foel Fenlli from the slopes of Moel Gyw

24

FOEL FENLLI to GARREG LWYD

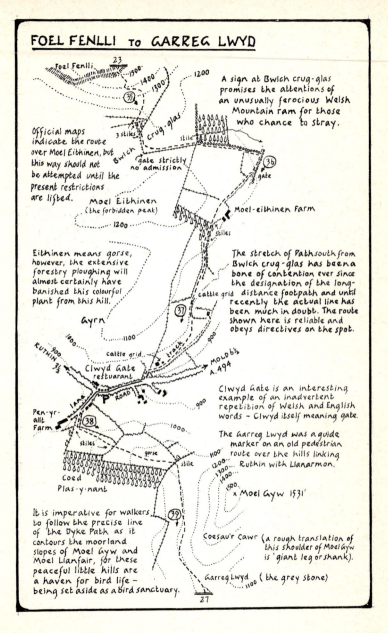

Foel Fenlli 23 1500 1400 1300 1200

35

A sign at Bwlch crug-glas promises the attentions of an unusually ferocious Welsh Mountain ram for those who chance to stray.

Official maps indicate the route over Moel Eithinen, but this way should not be attempted until the present restrictions are lifted.

3 stiles crug-glas stile

Bwlch gate strictly no admission

36 gate

Moel Eithinen (the forbidden peak)

Moel-eithinen Farm

1200 stiles

Eithinen means gorse, however, the extensive forestry ploughing will almost certainly have banished this colourful plant from this hill.

The stretch of Path south from Bwlch crug-glas has been a bone of contention ever since the designation of the long-distance footpath and until recently the actual line has been much in doubt. The route shown here is reliable and obeys directives on the spot.

cattle grid

37

Ayrn

1100 1400 900

RUTHIN 3½ 900 cattle grid track MOLD b½ A.494

Clwyd Gate restuarant

Clwyd Gate is an interesting example of an inadvertent repetition of Welsh and English words — Clwyd itself meaning gate.

ROAD 900

Pen-yr-allt Farm 38 1000

stiles gorse 1100 stile

The Garreg Lwyd was a guide marker on an old pedestrian route over the hills linking Ruthin with Llanarmon.

1200 1300 1400 1500

× Moel Gyw 1531'

Coed Plas-y-nant

It is imperative for walkers to follow the precise line of the Dyke Path as it contours the moorland slopes of Moel Gyw and Moel Llanfair, for these peaceful little hills are a haven for bird life — being set aside as a bird sanctuary.

39

Coesau'r Cawr (a rough translation of this shoulder of Moel Gyw is 'giant leg or shank).

Garreg Lwyd (the grey stone) 1100

27

25

Llanbedr Dyffryn Clwyd Church
in the background rises
Foel Fenlli

Clwyd Gate
Restaurant

The Raven Inn at
Llanarmon·yn·Ial

GARREG LWYD to MOEL Y GELLI

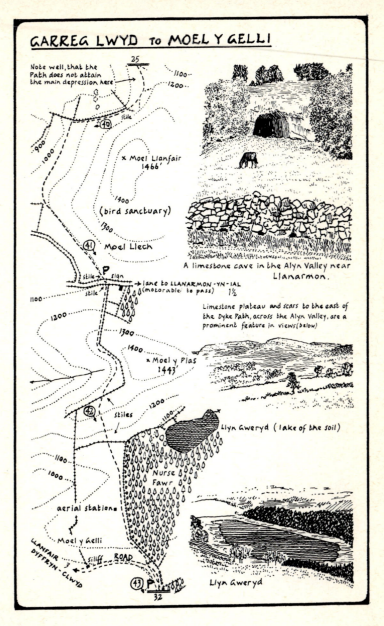

Note well, that the Path does not attain the main depression here →

25

1100
1200

49

stile

900
1000

✕ Moel Llanfair
1466'

1400

(bird sanctuary)

1300

41 Moel Llech

stile ⸱P sign

stile

→ lane to LLANARMON-YN-IAL
(motorable to pass) 1½

1100

1200

1300

1400

✕ Moel y Plas
1443'

42 stiles

1200

1100

1100

1000

Nurse Fawr

aerial station ▪

Moel y Gelli

LLANFAIR
DYFFRYN-CLWYD ← 3

Sliff ROAD

43 ⸱P

32

A limestone cave in the Alyn Valley near Llanarmon.

Limestone plateau and scars to the east of the Dyke Path, across the Alyn Valley, are a prominent feature in views (below)

Llyn Gweryd (lake of the soil)

Llyn Gweryd

27

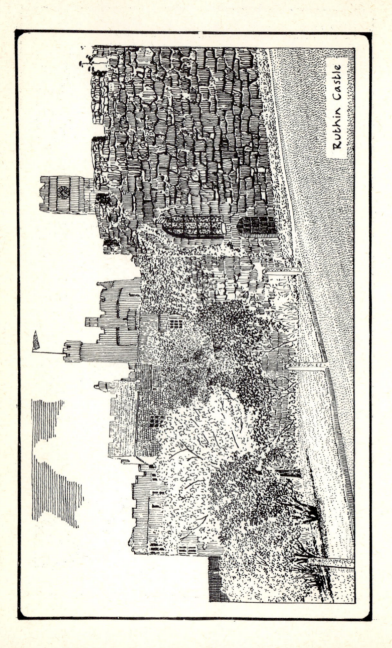

Ruthin Castle

Llanarmon-yn-Iâl, though one and a half miles east of the Path, is a good place to halt providing excellent accommodation particularly with reference to the Raven Inn (renown for the quality of its beer and cooking). Amid the principally stone built village there is a pretty double-aisled church dedicated to St. Garmon. Further, being in a limestone district, the scenery close by is worth seeking out.

Illustrated above is Mill Bridge over the river Alyn at Llanarmon, in the background is the limestone outcrop surmounted by Tomen-y-Faerdre (a castle mound). Iâl, pronounced 'Yarl', is a Welsh name meaning cultivated area.

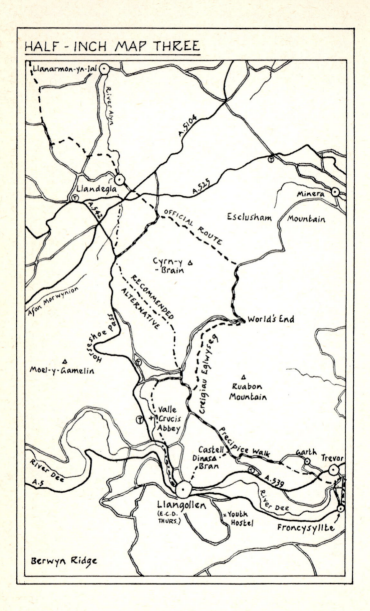

HALF - INCH MAP THREE

Llanarmon-yn-Ial

River Alyn

A.5104

A.525

Llandegla

A.542

Afon Morwynion

OFFICIAL ROUTE

Cyrn-y-Brain

RECOMMENDED ALTERNATIVE

Esclusham Mountain

Minera

World's End

Horseshoe Pass

Moel-y-Gamelin

Creigiau Eglwyseg

Ruabon Mountain

Valle Crucis Abbey

Precipice Walk

Castell Dinas Bran

Garth

Trevor

River Dee

A.5

A.539

River Dee

Llangollen
(E.C.D. THURS.)

×Youth Hostel

Froncysyllte

Berwyn Ridge

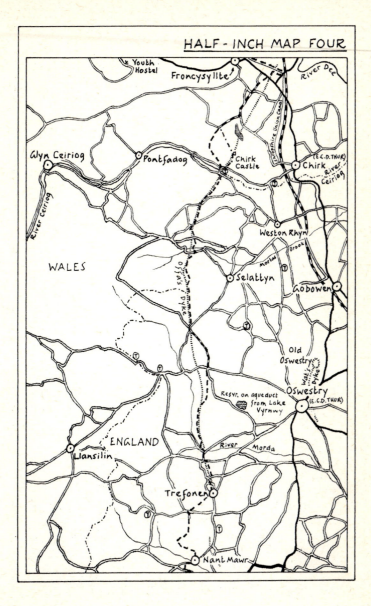

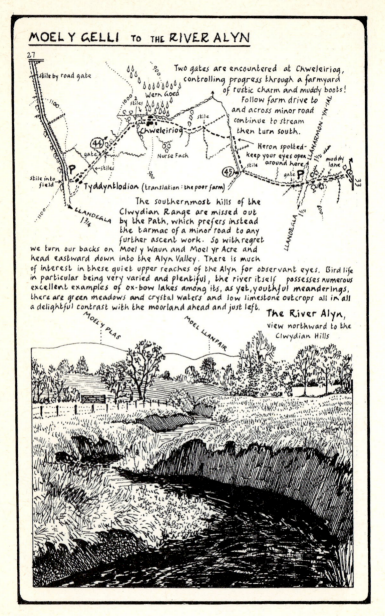

MOEL Y GELLI to the RIVER ALYN

27

stile by road gate

Two gates are encountered at Chweleiriog, controlling progress through a farmyard of rustic charm and muddy boots! Follow farm drive to and across minor road continue to stream then turn south.

Wern Goed

stiles

Chweleiriog

(44)

gate

stile

stile

Nurse Fach

Heron spotted— keep your eyes open around here

LLANARMON-YN-YAL

(45)

stile

gate

P

muddy lane

P

stile into field

stiles

33

Tyddyntlodion (translation: the poor farm)

LLANDEGLA 1¾

LLANDEGLA 1½

The southernmost hills of the Clwydian Range are missed out by the Path, which prefers instead the tarmac of a minor road to any further ascent work. So with regret we turn our backs on Moel y Waun and Moel yr Acre and head eastward down into the Alyn Valley. There is much of interest in these quiet upper reaches of the Alyn for observant eyes. Bird life in particular being very varied and plentiful, the river itself possesses numerous excellent examples of ox-bow lakes among its, as yet, youthful meanderings, there are green meadows and crystal waters and low limestone outcrops all in all a delightful contrast with the moorland ahead and just left.

The River Alyn, view northward to the Clwydian Hills

MOEL Y PLAS

MOEL LLANFAIR

RIVER ALYN to LLANDEGLA

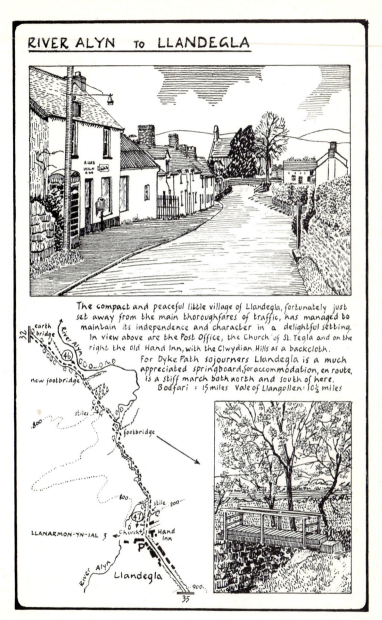

The compact and peaceful little village of Llandegla, fortunately just set away from the main thoroughfares of traffic, has managed to maintain its independence and character in a delightful setting. In view above are the Post Office, the Church of St. Tegla and on the right the old Hand Inn, with the Clwydian Hills as a backcloth.

For Dyke Path sojourners Llandegla is a much appreciated springboard, for accommodation, en route, is a stiff march both north and south of here.
Bodfari : 15 miles Vale of Llangollen : 10½ miles

earth bridge
32
River Alyn
46
new footbridge
stiles
800
footbridge
800
stile 800
47
LLANARMON-YN-IAL 3
Church
Hand Inn
P
River Alyn
Llandegla
900
35

Modernization does not necessarily mean improvement, however, Hafod Bilston has greatly benefited from a thorough renovation job, revitalising old stones in a refreshing manner. A unique piece of waymarking indicates the start of the next stage of our route – see gate below.

LLANDEGLA to HAFOD BILSTON

(above) The Hand Inn at Llandegla

The road is followed out of Llandegla to Pen-y-stryt (top of the street). Beyond the cross roads, where the road swings left, turn right and pass between the two new bungalows down onto the A.525, turn left along road and in 50 yds. cross a stile on the right. Descend and cross to a new footbridge into a particularly wet pasture, slant left to cross a fence which must be followed to a track leading to the road at Hafod Bilston.

Go through the well-marked gate before the stream, ascend to left of ravine and upon reaching the newly engineered track take the lower arm of the loop.

IMPORTANT

PLEASE TAKE NOTICE

Walkers planning to set out from Hafod Bilston must be prepared for hard going, the way over to the Minera - World's End road is fraught with physical and navigational obstacles not encountered anywhere else on the Dyke Path. The route is nowhere clear and in mist demands a practical knowledge in the use of map and compass of anyone contemplating this lonely crossing.

Hafod Bilston is an unusual and interesting group of buildings.

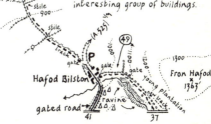

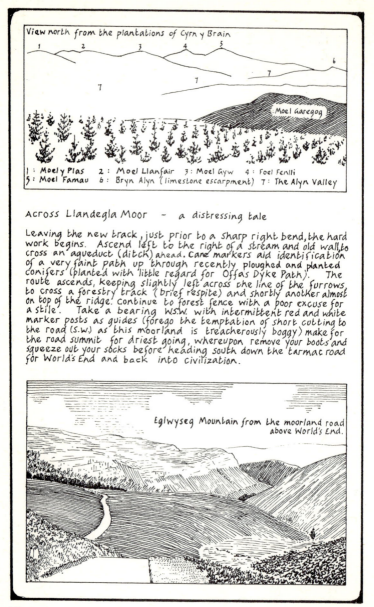

View north from the plantations of Cyrn y Brain

Moel Garegog

1 : Moel y Plas 2 : Moel Llanfair 3 : Moel Gyw 4 : Foel Fenlli
5 : Moel Famau 6 : Bryn Alyn (limestone escarpment) 7 : The Alyn Valley

Across Llandegla Moor - a distressing tale

Leaving the new track, just prior to a sharp right bend, the hard work begins. Ascend left to the right of a stream and old wall, to cross an aqueduct (ditch) ahead. Cane markers aid identification of a very faint path up through recently ploughed and planted conifers (planted with little regard for Offas Dyke Path). The route ascends, keeping slightly left across the line of the furrows, to cross a forestry track (brief respite) and shortly another almost on top of the ridge. Continue to forest fence with a poor excuse for a stile. Take a bearing W.S.W. with intermittent red and white marker posts as guides (forego the temptation of short cutting to the road (S.W.) as this moorland is treacherously boggy) make for the road summit for driest going, whereupon remove your boots and squeeze out your socks before heading south down the tarmac road for World's End and back into civilization.

Eglwyseg Mountain from the moorland road above World's End.

36

HAFOD BILSTON TO WORLD'S END

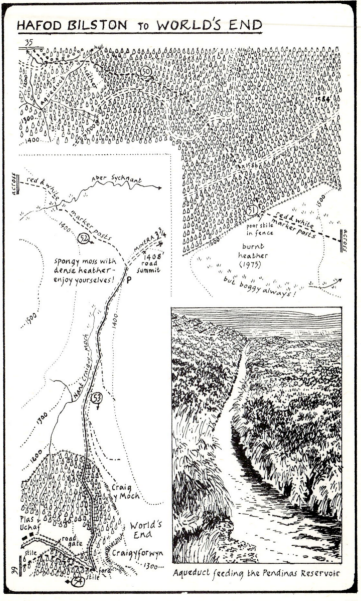

35

hut

aqueduct

1200
1300
1400
1500

50

1584

1586
1586

51

across

Aber Sychnant

fedd & white

marker posts

1300

52

spongy moss with
dense heather -
enjoy yourselves!

MINERA 2¾

1408'
road
summit

P

fedd white
marker posts

poor stile
in fence

burnt
heather
(1975)

but boggy always!

across

1600

1500

Nant Craig-y-Moch

1400

1300

53

1700

1800

Craig
y Moch

Plas
Uchaf

World's
End

road
gate

stile

Craigyforwyn

1300

39

ford

stile

54

Aqueduct feeding the Pendinas Reservoir

37

Plasuchaf, World's End

WORLD'S END to CRAIG ARTHUR

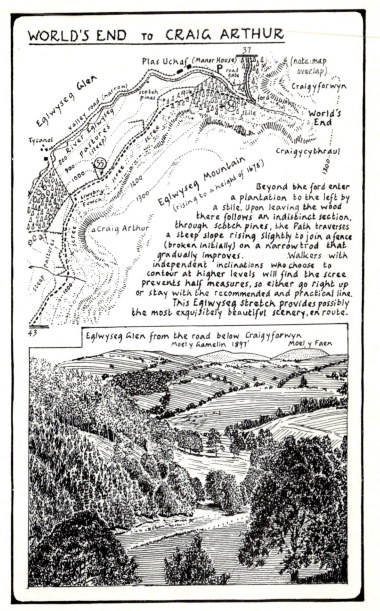

Eglwyseg Glen

valley road (narrow)

Tycanol

Plas Uchaf (Manor House)

37

P road gate

scotch pines

stile

54

stile

stile

ford

(note map overlap)

Craigyforwyn

World's End

Craigycythraul

River Eglwyseg

pastures (steep)

800
900
1000

55

Llwybr y Fwlch

1200

scree

Craig Arthur

scree

1300

Eglwyseg Mountain
(rising to a height of 1678')

1300

1200

1000

steep pastures

43

Beyond the ford enter a plantation to the left by a stile. Upon leaving the wood there follows an indistinct section, through scotch pines, the Path traverses a steep slope rising slightly to join a fence (broken initially) on a narrow trod that gradually improves.   Walkers with independent inclinations who choose to contour at higher levels will find the scree prevents half measures, so either go right up or stay with the recommended and practical line.
        This Eglwyseg stretch provides possibly the most exquisitely beautiful scenery, en route.

Eglwyseg Glen from the road below Craigyforwyn
Moel y Gamelin 1897'   Moel y Faen

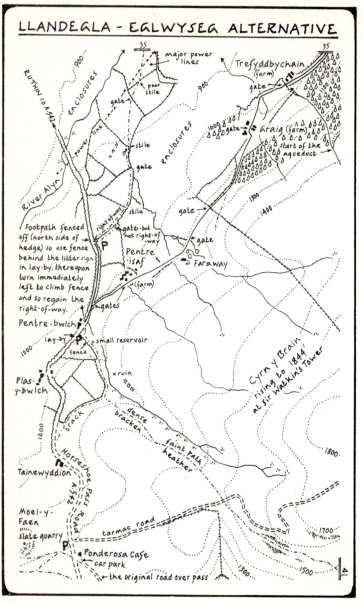

LLANDEGLA — EGLWYSEG ALTERNATIVE

RUTHIN 10 A.542

900

major power lines

35
35

Trefyddbychain (farm)

poor stile

gate

gate

enclosures

900

power line

gate

stile

enclosures

1000 gate

Graig (farm)

start of the aqueduct

gate

stile

gate

1300

1400

River Alyn

right-of-way

Footpath fenced off (north side of hedge) so use fence behind the litter sign in lay-by, thereupon turn immediately left to climb fence and so regain the right-of-way.

P

gate but not right-of-way

Pentre-isaf

gate

gate

Faraway

(farm)

gates

Pentre-bwlch

lay-by

P

small reservoir

1000

fence

x ruin

Cyrn y Brain rising to 1844' at Sir Watkin's Tower

900

Plas-y-bwlch

1200

track

dense bracken

faint path

heather

1800

Tainewyddion

Horseshoe Pass Road A.542

Moel-y-Faen slate quarry

tarmac road

1700

P

Ponderosa Cafe car park

1300

1500

← the original road over pass

41

40

Moel y Gamelin and
the Horseshoe Pass.

There are two practical starts
(between Llandegla and A.542)
to this link route. Either follow
the main route to Hafod Bilston
there continuing along the rough
tarmac gated road, or, preferably,
use the field paths. Although the
rights-of-way are in a poor state
of repair, especially where it meets
the A542, and despite some fields
being liable to cultivation, it is
better to use this route rather than
be subject to too much road walking.

The ascent from Pentre-bwlch
deteriorates when the track is
left above the intakes, waist high
bracken is followed by knee deep
heather eventually, however, the Radio
Station (private) road is crossed with
the best now upon you with a delightful
shelf path above a steep drop giving
exquisite views to south and west.

The views of Moel-y-Gamelin and
later of World's End and Eglwyseg
Glen coupled with the comparative
ease in route finding gives this route
the edge over the official way plodding,
as it does, through the bogs and
plantations across Llandegla Moor.

Map labels:
1400 · clear path · 40
1300 · Caer Hafod ruin · 1200 · 1100 · Nant Alas · old slate quarry
pass through two gates in sheep pens
track
green lane
ruins
"a solitary abode" · Glyn (cottage) · fences
Aber-gwern · old slate quarry
1200 · 1000 · gate

43

Two views of
Creigiau Eglwyseg
and Craig Arthur

CRAIG ARTHUR to TANYCASTELL

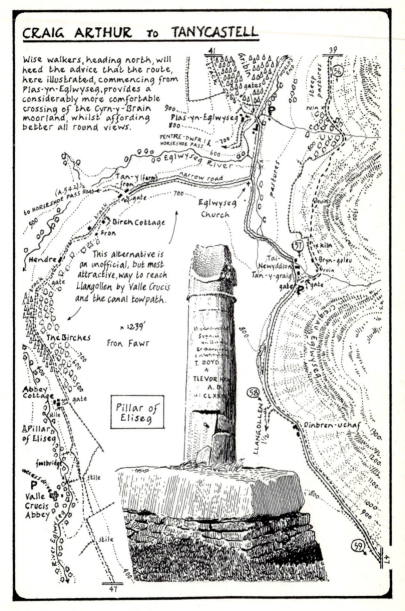

Wise walkers, heading north, will heed the advice that the route, here illustrated, commencing from Plas-yn-Eglwyseg, provides a considerably more comfortable crossing of the Cyrn-y-Brain moorland, whilst affording better all round views.

This alternative is an unofficial, but most attractive, way to reach Llangollen by Valle Crucis and the canal towpath.

Plas-yn-Eglwyseg

PENTRE-DWFR &
HORSESHOE PASS

Eglwyseg River

Tan-y (farm)
fron

narrow road

(A.542) 2½
to HORSESHOE PASS ROAD

gate

Eglwyseg
Church

Birch Cottage
Fron

Hendre

gate

The Birches

Abbey
Cottage
gate
stile

A Pillar
of Eliseg

footbridge
stile

P

Valle
Crucis
Abbey

stile

× 1239'
Fron Fawr

Pillar of
Eliseg

sheep
pastures

ruin

pastures

Kiln
Bryn-goleu
ruin

Tai-
Newyddion
Tan-y-graig
gate   gate

Dinbren-uchaf

Llangollen
1½

47

43

Valle Crucis Abbey

Castell Dinas Bran

Those who climb to the top of this little hill are blessed by the joy of a heaven of their very own, a complete panorama of hills, a blaze of colour. To the north the dark moors of Cyrn-y-Brain 1844' (top illustration) contrast with the gleaming white cliffs of Creigiau Eglwyseg. The bracken clad Llantysilio Mountain (bottom illustration) contrasting with the green woods and pastures leads the eye down to the river meadows and canal far below. Southward the fair Vale of Llangollen backed by the northern outposts of the Berwyn Range. So much beauty for such little effort.

Dee Bridge, Llangollen

Castell Dinas Bran and Trefor Rocks

LLANGOLLEN and the PRECIPICE WALK

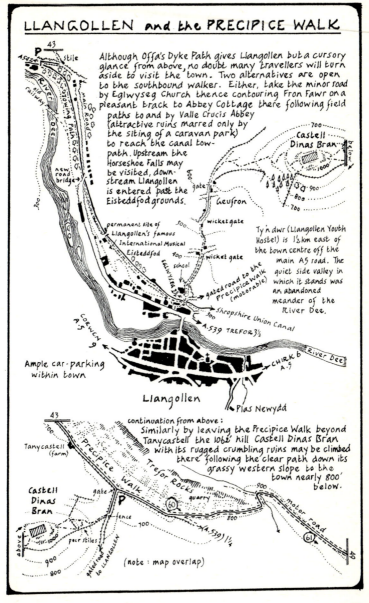

Although Offa's Dyke Path gives Llangollen but a cursory glance from above, no doubt many travellers will turn aside to visit the town. Two alternatives are open to the southbound walker. Either, take the minor road by Eglwyseg Church thence contouring Fron Fawr on a pleasant track to Abbey Cottage there following field paths to and by Valle Crucis Abbey (attractive ruins marred only by the siting of a caravan park) to reach the canal towpath. Upstream the Horseshoe Falls may be visited, downstream Llangollen is entered past the Eisteddfod grounds.

permanent site of Llangollen's famous International Musical Eisteddfod

Ty'n dwr (Llangollen Youth Hostel) is 1½ km east of the town centre off the main A5 road. The quiet side valley in which it stands was an abandoned meander of the River Dee.

Ample car-parking within town

Llangollen

continuation from above:
Similarly by leaving the Precipice Walk beyond Tanycastell the 1062' hill Castell Dinas Bran with its rugged crumbling ruins may be climbed there following the clear path down its grassy western slope to the town nearly 800' below.

Tanycastell (farm)

Castell Dinas Bran

(note: map overlap)

47

The old Cysyllte Bridge and Thomas Telford's early 19th century Pontcysyllte Aqueduct.

PRECIPICE WALK TO FRONCYSYLLTE

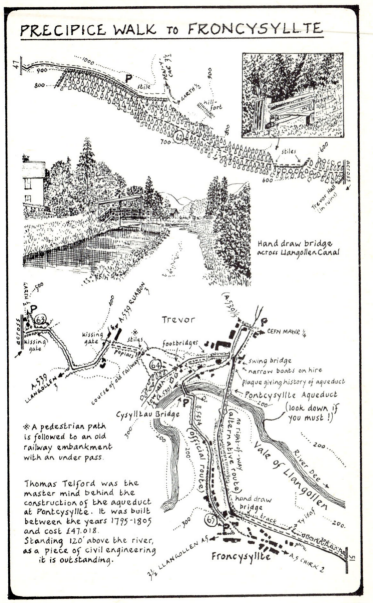

Hand draw bridge across Llangollen Canal

Trevor

CEFN MAWR ½

swing bridge
narrow boats on hire
plaque giving history of aqueduct
Pontcysyllte Aqueduct
(look down if you must!)

Vale of Llangollen

River Dee →

Cysylltau Bridge

※ A pedestrian path is followed to an old railway embankment with an under pass.

Thomas Telford was the master mind behind the construction of the aqueduct at Pontcysyllte. It was built between the years 1795-1805 and cost £47.018.
Standing 120' above the river, as a piece of civil engineering it is outstanding.

Froncysyllte

hand draw bridge

2½ LLANGOLLEN A5

A5 CHIRK 2

49

Offa's Dyke converging with the Shropshire Union Canal, in the background a multi-arched railway viaduct spans the wide Dee valley.

Plas Offa

FRONCYSYLLTE TO CAEAU-GWYNION

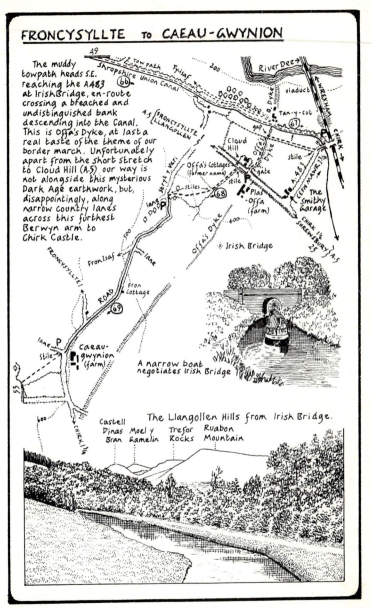

The muddy towpath heads S.E. reaching the A483 at Irish Bridge, en-route crossing a breached and undistinguished bank descending into the Canal. This is Offa's Dyke, at last a real taste of the theme of our border march. Unfortunately apart from the short stretch to Cloud Hill (A.5) our way is not alongside this mysterious Dark Age earthwork, but, disappointingly, along narrow country lanes across this furthest Berwyn arm to Chirk Castle.

49

Shropshire Union Canal   Tow path   Ty-isaf   200   River Dee→

66   Offa's Dyke   WREXHAM   viaduct   Tan-y-cut

A.5 (FRONCYSYLLTE / LLANGOLLEN)   gap   67   CHIRK

Cloud Hill   Offa's Dyke   stile   CEFN MAWR 1½m

Offa's Cottages (former name)   gate   A.483   The Smithy Garage

lane   Lôn yr y fron   stile   Plas-Offa (farm)   CHIRK 1½ SHREWSBURY 2½

68   O. stiles

lane   O DDU   400   Offa's Dyke   ✕ Irish Bridge

600   Fronisaf   lane

FRONCYSYLLTE   ROAD   Fron Cottage

69

lane   P   Caeau-gwynion (farm)   A narrow boat negotiates Irish Bridge

stile   600   CHIRK 1½   55

The Llangollen Hills from Irish Bridge.

Castell Dinas Bran   Moel y Gamelin   Trefor Rocks   Ruabon Mountain

The romantic era which made it fashionable to visit parts of Wales, brought with it a refinement in the appreciation of beauty and scenery (sadly missing today). Included among the so called "Seven Wonders of Wales" were the Chirk Castle gates (ornamental wrought-iron gates and screen), made in 1719-21 by two local blacksmiths. Originally they stood on the north front of the castle, but were moved in 1770. Chirk Castle, still a family home, is open to the public during summer months and is well worth including in modern intineraries too.

Chirk Castle – north front minus metal railings

The Vale of Llangollen from the Berwyn ridge above Chirk Castle. In view are :-

A : Castell Dinas Bran 1020'   B : Moel Morfydd 1802'
C : Moel y Gamelin 1897'   D : Moel y Faen 1500'+
E : Creigiau Eglwyseg   F : Ruabon Mountain 1678'

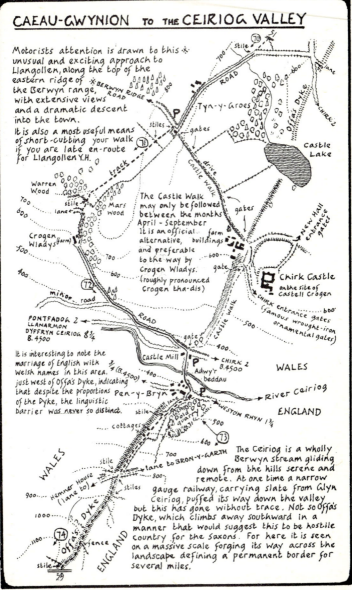

CAEAU-GWYNION to the CEIRIOG VALLEY

Motorists attention is drawn to this ☀ unusual and exciting approach to Llangollen, along the top of the eastern ridge of the Berwyn range, with extensive views and a dramatic descent into the town.

It is also a most useful means of short-cutting your walk if you are late en-route for Llangollen Y.H.

Warren Wood

Mars Wood

Crogen Wladys (farm)

The Castle Walk may only be followed between the months April – September. It is an official alternative, farm buildings and preferable to the way by Crogen Wladys. (roughly pronounced Crogen tha-dis)

BERWYN RIDGE ROAD

ROAD

Tyn-y-Groes

OFFA'S DYKE

CHIRK 2

Castle Lake

Castle Walk

drive

gates

New Hall entrance gates

Chirk Castle
on the site of Castell Crogen

CHIRK entrance gates 600' (famous wrought-iron ornamental gates)

minor road

ROAD

PONTFADOG 2
LLANARMON
DYFFRYN CEIRIOG 8¼
B. 4500

It is interesting to note the marriage of English with Welsh names in this area, just west of Offa's Dyke, indicating that despite the proportions of the Dyke, the linguistic barrier was never so distinct.

Castle Walk

gate

Castle Mill

Adwy'r beddau

CHIRK 2
B. 4500

WALES

Pen-y-Bryn

WESTON RHYN 1¾

River Ceiriog

ENGLAND

cottages

lane to BRON-Y-GARTH

WALES

Hamner House (lane to)

Offa's Dyke

ENGLAND

The Ceiriog is a wholly Berwyn stream gliding down from the hills serene and remote. At one time a narrow gauge railway, carrying slate from Glyn Ceiriog, puffed its way down the valley but this has gone without trace. Not so Offa's Dyke, which climbs away southward in a manner that would suggest this to be hostile country for the Saxons. For here it is seen on a massive scale forging its way across the landscape defining a permanent border for several miles.

Chirk Castle from across the Ceiriog Valley

Offa's Dyke

(illustration above)
Offa's Dyke runs through the grounds of and close to Chirk Castle, as may be seen in the view above.

The Castle, which is rectangular in plan, was built by Roger de Mortimer during the time of Edward I, on the site of a much older fortification - Castell Crogen, a name that still survives hereabouts, an example being the farm Crogen Wladys on the official path near by.

(illustration left)
Bridge over River Ceiriog, strangely the border fails to maintain its line coming northward with Offa's Dyke, for at Pen-y-Bryn it slants off to join the river a short distance to the east of this bridge.

54

Offa's Dyke and Chirk Castle

Castle Mill, Church and footpath to Chirk Castle

The drawings shown here give some idea of the present
state of Offa's Dyke immediately south of the Ceiriog valley.

C19th wayside monument near Craignant

CEIRIOG VALLEY TO CRAIGNANT

Selattyn Church

Selattyn Hill from the Dyke by Plas Crogen

Map annotations (clockwise):

53
BRON-Y-GARTH
2 stiles
(B.4579) 1½
1000
Nant Eris (ravine)
footbridge & 2 stiles
2 stiles
1100
old lane (overgrown)
BRON-Y-GARTH 1¼
horse
Plas Crogen (farm)
stile
QUINTA 1½
(B.4579) ½
3 stiles
1200
gate
P 1100
minor road
1000
(B.4579) ½
monument to Offa's Dyke
old quarry
Craignant (farm)
mine road
GLYN CEIRIOG B.4579 3½
1000
gate SELATTYN 1
Morlas Brook
track
old quarry
gate
76
to Birch Cottage
61

59

Oswestry Old Racecourse

Baker's Hill (no path)

Offa's Dyke approaching Carreg-y-Big Farm
(the Path follows the road trending away from the Dyke)

Llangollen (directly beyond) and Dee Valley

Craig-y-dduallt

View north from Offa's Dyke as it crosses the shoulder of Selattyn Hill

CRAIGNANT to CARREG-Y-BIG

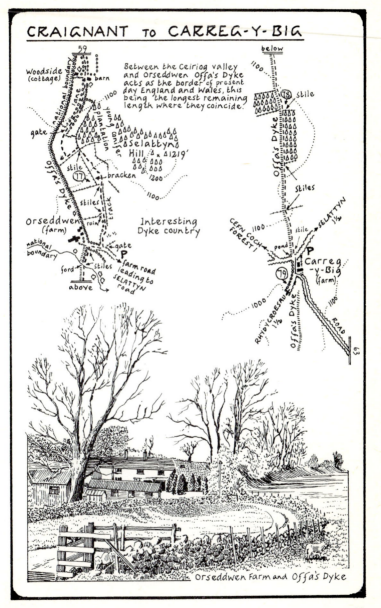

Between the Ceiriog valley and Orseddwen Offa's Dyke acts as the border of present day England and Wales, this being the longest remaining length where they coincide.

Woodside (cottage)

59

barn

gate

national boundary

young conifer plantation

Offa's Dyke

stile 77

bracken

Selattyn Hill △ 1219'

1200

1100

stiles

track

ruin

Orseddwen (farm)

national boundary

gate

P

farm road leading to SELATTYN road

ford

stiles

above

Interesting Dyke country

below

1100

78 stile

Offa's Dyke

Stiles

CEFN COCH (FOREST)

1100

stile

SELATTYN ½

pond

P

Carreg -y-Big (farm)

79

RHYDYCROESAU ½

Offa's Dyke

1000

1100

ROAD

63

Orseddwen Farm and Offa's Dyke

61

Offa's Dyke Path running alongside the Dyke through Llanforda Woods – note seat recessed into earthwork just to the south of Craig Forda (see inset above).

Gyrn Moelfre
1715'

Mynydd
Lledrod
1356'

Cadair Fronwen
2572'

OFFA'S
DYKE

BERWYN MOUNTAINS

Baker's Hill

Forced away from the Dyke at Carreg-y-Big the Path takes a second best route along a minor road to Oswestry Old Racecourse, whereupon a view opens up to the west rivalling any on our border trek.

CARREG·Y·BIG TO CRAIG FORDA

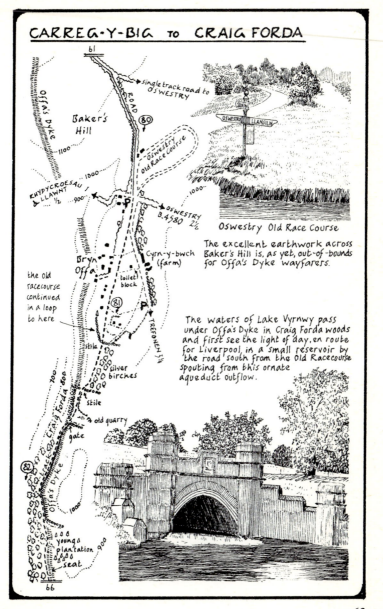

61

single track road to OSWESTRY

ROAD

Baker's Hill

80

Offa's Dyke

1100

Oswestry Old Race Course

1000

RHYDYCROESAU & LLAWNT ½

900

1000

OSWESTRY B.4580 2½

Oswestry Old Race Course

The excellent earthwork across Baker's Hill is, as yet, out-of-bounds for Offa's Dyke wayfarers.

Cyrn-y-bwch (farm)

Bryn Offa

toilet block

the old racecourse continued in a loop to here

81

TREFONEN 3¾

The waters of Lake Vyrnwy pass under Offa's Dyke in Craig Forda woods and first see the light of day, en route for Liverpool, in a small reservoir by the road south from the Old Racecourse spouting from this ornate aqueduct outflow.

stile

silver birches

900   800

track to Craig Forda

stile

old quarry

gate

82

Offa's Dyke

1000

900

young plantation

seat

66

63

← WAT'S DYKE

Old Oswestry (Hen Domen) is something of an eye catcher so far as Iron-age hill-forts go. Built on a natural moraine, yet giving the impression of being man-made, the great ramparts cannot fail to stir the imagination and to walk round the upper tier is a popular excursion enjoyed by Oswestry folk. Wat's Dyke was aligned to it and can be seen on this drawing, taken from the Wat's Dyke recreation park, emerging from the south-western corner of the fort. The exact origins of Wat's Dyke have remained a mystery to historians without doc-umentary evidence to support theories of its age, purpose and builders; however, it has been assumed to be a pre-Offan Mercian earthwork, a first tentative attempt to fix a frontier - this being a tradition later expanded on by King Offa.

Morda Valley and Lianforda Wood

OFFA'S DYKE →

One of the delights of following Offa's Dyke is the way it can appear suddenly as a great earthwork of startling proportions and then fall away abruptly as an insignificant hedge-bank with no ditch. The two illustrations above give some idea of this along the Dykes course just north of Trefonen.

65

CRAIG FORDA to TY-CANOL

Special care is required at the point marked 'A', where pig enclosures have hindered the route into Trefonen.

A particularly pleasant stretch of Path is that through the woods from Craig Forda to the Morda Valley.

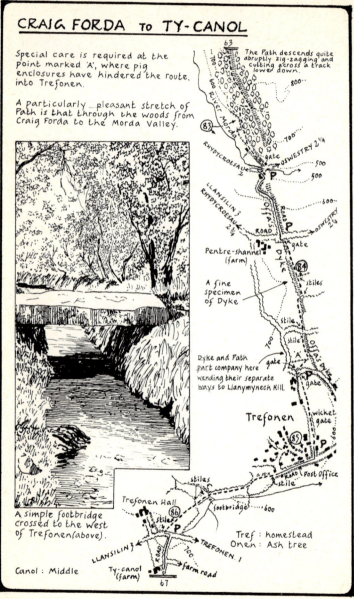

The Path descends quite abruptly zig-zagging and cutting across a track lower down.

800

700

600

83

RIVER MORDA

RHYDYCROESAU 2

gate

OSWESTRY 2¼

500

500

P

600

LLANSILIN 3
RHYDYCROESAU 2¼

ROAD

P

OSWESTRY 2½

ROAD

gate

Pentre-shannel (farm)

84

A fine specimen of Dyke

stiles

stile

700

stile

stile

OFFA'S

Dyke and Path part company here wending their separate ways to Llanymynech Hill.

gate

'A'

gate

Trefonen

wicket gate

85

P

600

stile

ROAD

Post Office

stiles

Trefonen Hall

footbridge

600

86

stile

P

TREFONEN 1

LLANSILIN 3

ROAD

700

farm road

Ty-canol (farm)

67

A simple footbridge crossed to the west of Trefonen (above).

Tref: homestead
Onen: Ash tree

Canol: Middle

TY-CANOL TO PORTH-Y-WAEN

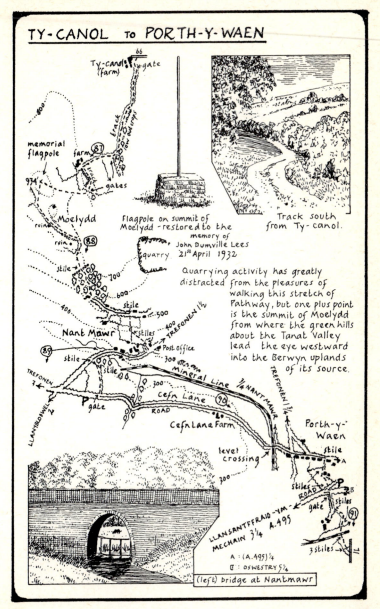

Ty-Canol (farm)

66

gate

memorial flagpole

800

track

(low but steep)

farm 87

974

gates

Moelydd

ruin

ruin

88

stile

700

800

stile

600

Nant Mawr

500

stiles

400

TREFONEN 1½

89

stile

Post office

300 yds approx

stile

Mineral Line

¼ NANT MAWR

TREFONEN ¼

LLANBLODWEL 2

TREFONEN 2

gate

ROAD

Cefn Lane

90

Cefn Lane Farm

level crossing

300

Porth-y-Waen

stile

A

stiles

P

B

gate

stiles

91

3 stiles

Flagpole on summit of Moelydd – restored to the memory of John Dumville Lees 21st April 1932

Track south from Ty-canol.

Quarrying activity has greatly distracted from the pleasures of walking this stretch of Pathway, but one plus point is the summit of Moelydd from where the green hills about the Tanat Valley lead the eye westward into the Berwyn uplands of its source.

LLANSANTFFRAID-YM-MECHAIN 3¼

A.495

A : (A.495) ¼
B : OSWESTRY 5¼

(left) bridge at Nantmawr

67

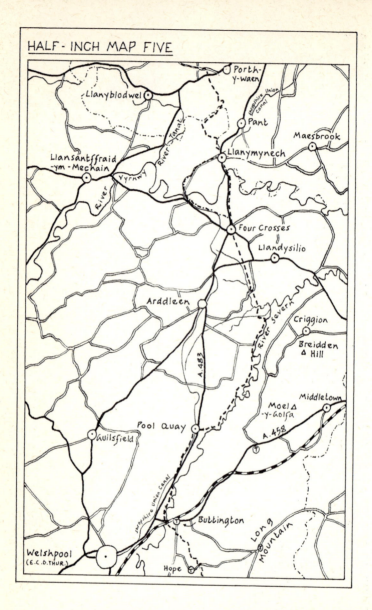

HALF-INCH MAP FIVE

Porth-y-waen

Llanyblodwel

Pant

Maesbrook

Llansantffraid-ym-Mechain

River Tanat

River Vyrnwy

Llanymynech

Shropshire Union Canal

Four Crosses

Llandysilio

Arddleen

River Severn

Criggion

Breidden △ Hill

A.483

Moel △ -y-Golfa

Middletown

Pool Quay

A.458

Ⓣ

Guilsfield

Shropshire Union Canal

Long Mountain

Welshpool
(E.C.D.THUR.)

Buttington

Hope

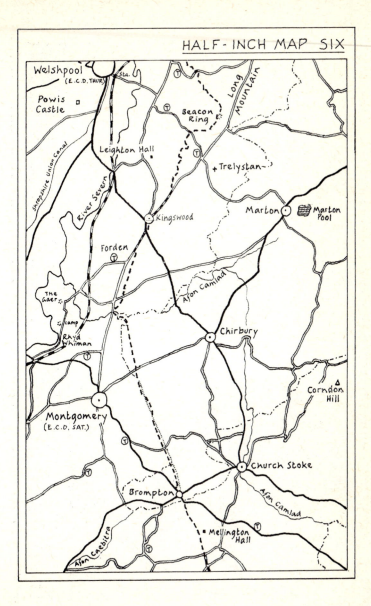

Welshpool
(E.C.D.THUR.) Sta.

Powis
Castle

Shropshire Union Canal

River Severn

Long Mountain

Beacon
Ring

Leighton Hall

Trelystan

Kingswood

Marton

Marton
Pool

Forden

Afon Camlad

The
Gaer

camp

Rhyd
Whiman

Chirbury

Corndon
Hill

Montgomery
(E.C.D. SAT.)

Church Stoke

Brompton

Afon Camlad

Mellington
Hall

Afon Caebitra

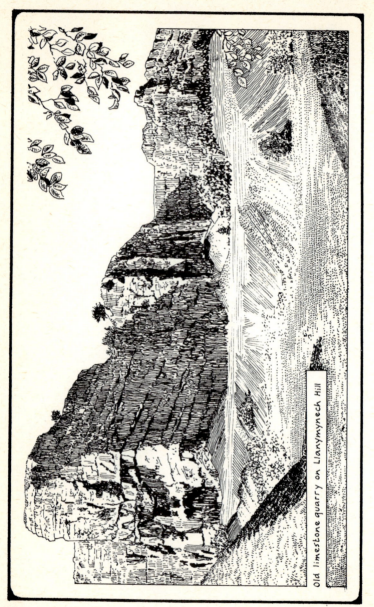

Old limestone quarry on Llanymynech Hill

PORTH-Y-WAEN TO LLANYMYNECH

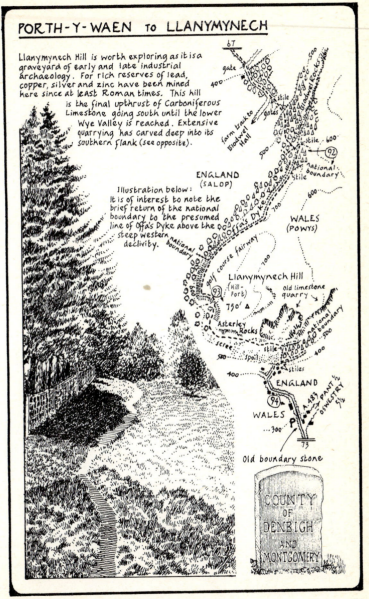

Llanymynech Hill is worth exploring as it is a graveyard of early and late industrial archaeology. For rich reserves of lead, copper, silver and zinc have been mined here since at least Roman times. This hill is the final upthrust of Carboniferous Limestone going south until the lower Wye Valley is reached. Extensive quarrying has carved deep into its southern flank (see opposite).

Illustration below:
It is of interest to note the brief return of the national boundary to the presumed line of Offa's Dyke above the steep western declivity.

67

gate

400

Blodwel Rocks

stile

gates

farm track to Blodwel Hall

500

stile 600

92

national boundary

ENGLAND (SALOP)

stile

600

700

Offa's Dyke

WALES (POWYS)

national boundary

golf course fairway

700

Llanymynech Hill (Hill-Fort)

93

750' △

old limestone quarry

national boundary

Asterley Rocks

scree

700

stile

spoil

500

700

400

stiles

ENGLAND

A483 PANT ½ OSWESTRY 5¼

94

WALES

300

73

Old boundary stone

COUNTY OF DENBIGH AND MONTGOMERY

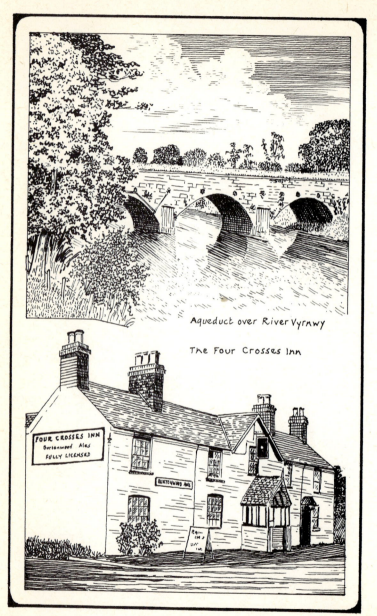

Aqueduct over River Vyrnwy

The Four Crosses Inn

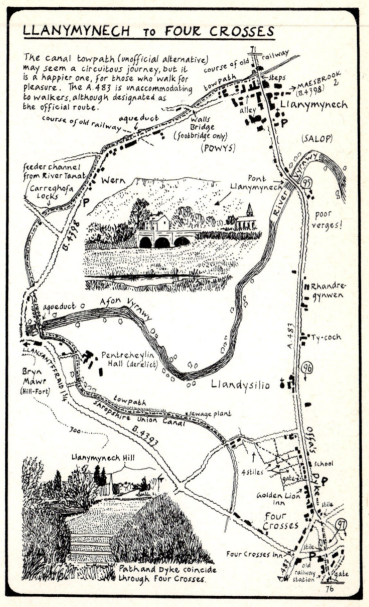

LLANYMYNECH TO FOUR CROSSES

The canal towpath (unofficial alternative) may seem a circuitous journey, but it is a happier one, for those who walk for pleasure. The A.483 is unaccommodating to walkers, although designated as the official route.

course of old railway

aqueduct

course of old railway

Walls Bridge (footbridge only)
(POWYS)

feeder channel from River Tanat

Carreghofa Locks

Wern

P

B.4398

course of old railway

towpath

steps

MAESBROOK (B.4398) 2

alley

Llanymynech

(SALOP)

Pont Llanymynech

River Vyrnwy

95

poor verges!

Rhandregynwen

aqueduct

Afon Vyrnwy

A.483

Ty-coch

96

LLANSANTFFRAID 1¼

Pentreheylin Hall (derelict)

Llandysilio

Bryn Mawr (Hill-Fort)

towpath

Shropshire Union Canal

B.4393

sewage plant

300

Offa's Dyke

Llanymynech Hill

4 stiles

gate

school

Golden Lion Inn

Four Crosses

stile

97

Four Crosses Inn

stile

P

A.483

old railway station

gate

Path and Dyke coincide through Four Crosses.

76

73

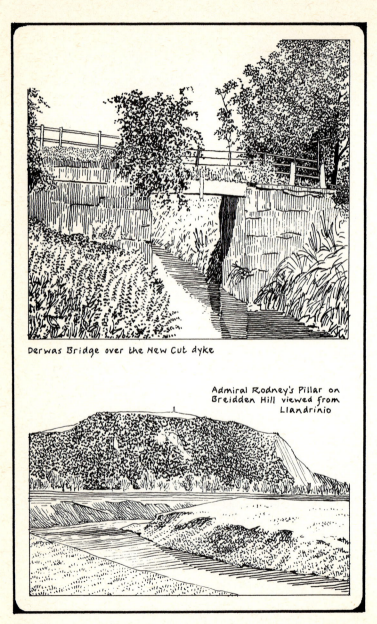

Derwas Bridge over the New Cut dyke

Admiral Rodney's Pillar on
Breidden Hill viewed from
Llandrinio

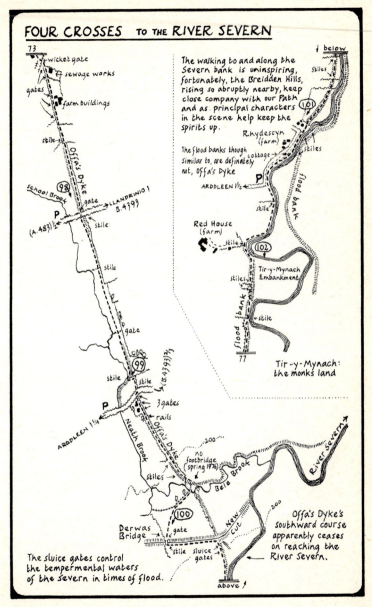

FOUR CROSSES TO THE RIVER SEVERN

73

wicket gate
sewage works
gates
farm buildings
stile
Offa's Dyke
School Brook
98
gate
LLANDRINIO 1
B.4393
P
(A.483) ½
stile
stile
stile
gate
99
(B.4393) ⅔
stile
stile
P
3 gates
rails
ARDDLEEN 1¼
Neath Brook
Offa's Dyke
stiles
no footbridge
(spring 1976)
Beie Brook
200
100
gate
Derwas Bridge
stile
sluice gates
New Cut
200
River Severn

The walking to and along the
Severn bank is uninspiring,
fortunately, the Breidden Hills,
rising so abruptly nearby, keep
close company with our Path
and as principal characters
in the scene help keep the
spirits up.

The flood banks though
similar to, are definately
not, Offa's Dyke

ARDDLEEN 1½

↑ below
stiles
101
Rhydescyn
(farm)
cottage
stiles
P
stile
Red House
(farm)
stile
102
Tir-y-Mynach
Embankment
stiles
stile
flood bank
77

Tir-y-Mynach:
the monks land

flood bank

Offa's Dyke's
southward course
apparently ceases
on reaching the
River Severn.

The sluice gates control
the tempermental waters
of the Severn in times of flood.

above ↑

75

Lock on the Shropshire Union Canal at Pool Quay.

Moel y Golfa from the bridge abutments by the Severn

76

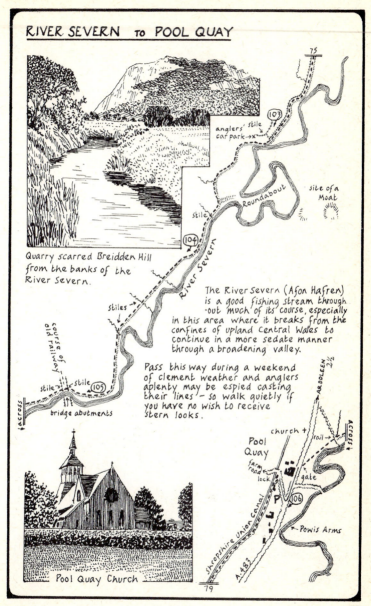

RIVER SEVERN to POOL QUAY

75

103

anglers' stile
car park →×—×

site of a Moat

Roundabout

stile

104

River Severn

Quarry scarred Breidden Hill from the banks of the River Severn.

Stiles →

course of old railway

stile — stile
105
← across
bridge abutments

The River Severn (Afon Hafren) is a good fishing stream through-out much of its course, especially in this area where it breaks from the confines of upland Central Wales to continue in a more sedate manner through a broadening valley.

Pass this way during a weekend of clement weather and anglers aplenty may be espied casting their lines — so walk quietly if you have no wish to receive stern looks.

ARDLEEN 2½

church + trail
← ACROSS →

Pool Quay

farm road
lock

gate

106

Shropshire Union Canal

A.483

← Powis Arms

Pool Quay Church

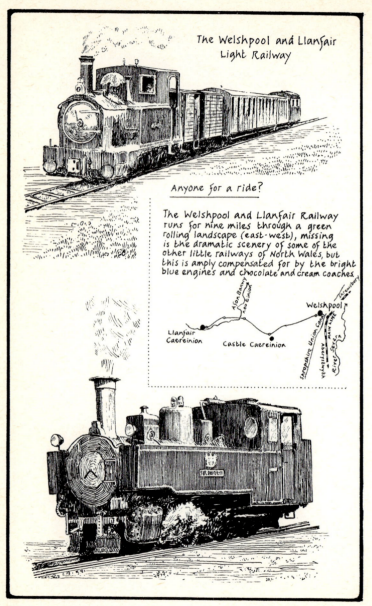

The Welshpool and Llanfair Light Railway

Anyone for a ride?

The Welshpool and Llanfair Railway runs for nine miles through a green rolling landscape (east-west), missing is the dramatic scenery of some of the other little railways of North Wales, but this is amply compensated for by the bright blue engines and chocolate and cream coaches

POOL QUAY to BUTTINGTON

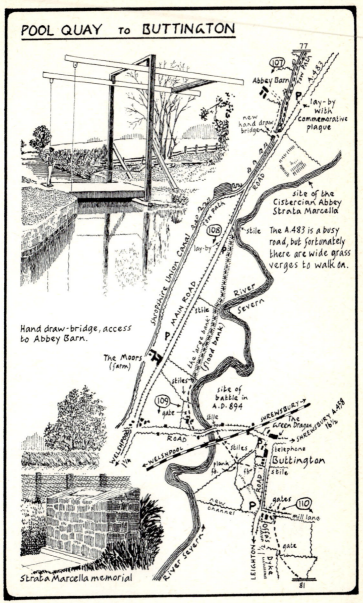

Hand draw-bridge, access to Abbey Barn.

Strata Marcella memorial

Map labels:

77

107

Abbey Barn

P lay-by with commemorative plaque

new hand draw bridge

Tow Path

A.483

site of the Cistercian Abbey Strata Marcella

108

stile

The A.483 is a busy road, but fortunately there are wide grass verges to walk on.

lay-by

Shropshire Union Canal A.D. 1811

Tow Path

MAIN ROAD

ROAD

stile

River Severn

The large bank (flood bank)

P

The Moors (farm)

stiles

109

gate

site of battle in A.D. 894

stile

SHREWSBURY

SHREWSBURY A.458

The Green Dragon

SHREWSBURY 16½

WELSHPOOL 1¼

WELSHPOOL ROAD

stiles

plank f.b.

f.b.

telephone

Buttington

stile

new channel

P

gates

110

mill lane

LEIGHTON 1¼

OFFA'S

ROAD

Dyke

gate

81

79

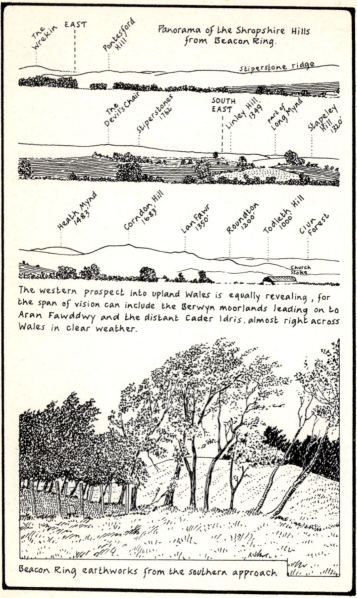

Panorama of the Shropshire Hills from Beacon Ring.

The Wrekin EAST

Pontesford Hill

stiperstone ridge

The Devil's Chair

Stiperstones 1762

SOUTH EAST

Linley Hill 1349

part of Long Mynd

Stapeley Hill 1320'

Heath Mynd 1483'

Corndon Hill 1683'

Lan Fawr 1350'

Roundton 1200'

Todleth Hill 1000'

Clun Forest

Church Stoke

The western prospect into upland Wales is equally revealing, for the span of vision can include the Berwyn moorlands leading on to Aran Fawddwy and the distant Cader Idris, almost right across Wales in clear weather.

Beacon Ring earthworks from the southern approach

BUTTINGTON to PANT-Y-BWCH

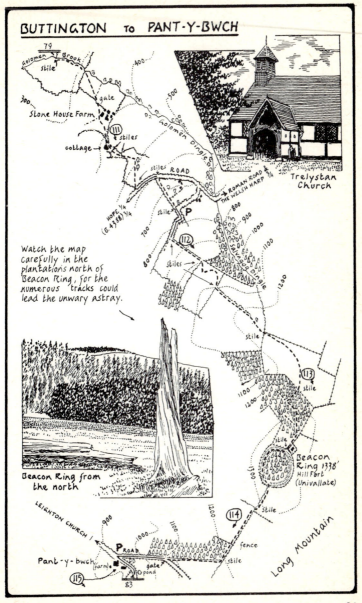

79

Kolomen Brook
stile
400
500
300
Kolomen Dingle
Stone House Farm
gate
111 stiles
cottage

stiles ROAD
stile
HOPE ¼
(6.438) ³/₄
700
800
P
112
stiles
Roman Road ½
The Welsh Harp
800
900
1000
1100
Kolwyddan Dingle
1200

Watch the map
carefully in the
plantations north of
Beacon Ring, for the
numerous tracks could
lead the unwary astray.

Trelystan
Church

stile
stile
113
1100
1200
Beacon
Ring 1338'
Hill Fort
(Univallate)
1300

Beacon Ring from
the north

stile
900
1200
LEIGHTON CHURCH 1
1000
1100
114
fence
stile
P ROAD
gate
Pant-y-bwch (farm)
pond
115
83
Long Mountain

81

Reservoir below Pant y Bwch Farm

Moel y Mab

Leighton Park Farm

82

PANT-Y-BWCH TO KINGSWOOD

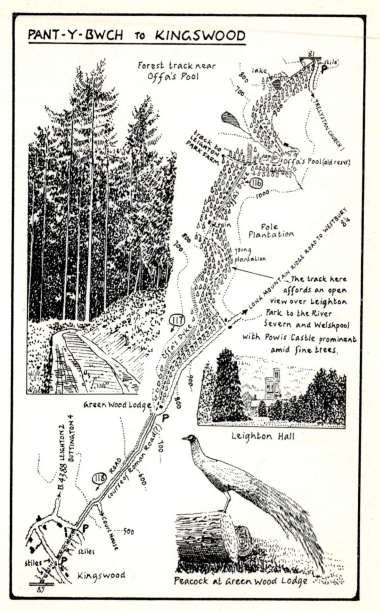

Forest track near Offa's Pool

81
stile
P
lake
800
700
TRELYSTAN CHURCH 1

track to LEIGHTON PARK FARM

dam

Offa's Pool (old resvr.)

116

1000

Offa's Dyke

800

ruin

700

Pole Plantation

young plantation

LONG MOUNTAIN RIDGE ROAD TO WESTBURY 8¼

The track here affords an open view over Leighton Park to the River Severn and Welshpool with Powis Castle prominent amid fine trees.

117

Offa's Dyke

900

Green Wood Lodge

800

P

Leighton Hall

LEIGHTON 2
BUTTINGTON 4

B 4388

ROAD

118

Course of Roman Road (?)

700

600

500

Court House

P

stiles

stiles

P

Kingswood

85

Peacock at Green Wood Lodge

83

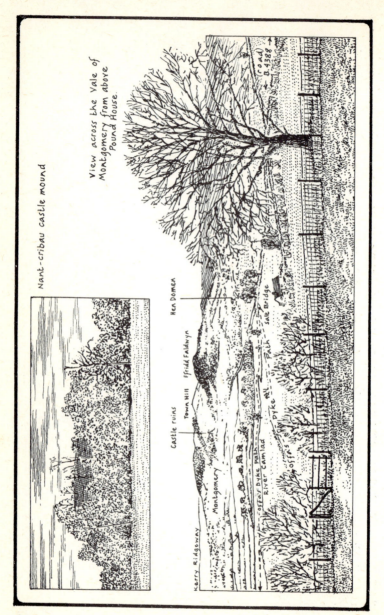

Nant-cribau castle mound

View across the Vale of Montgomery from above Pound House.

Castle ruins

Town Hill   Efrid Faldwyn

Hen Domen

Kerry Ridgeway

Montgomery

Offa's Dyke Path

River Camlad

Dyke Pll

Path

Offa's

Sale Bridge

(road)
B.4388

N

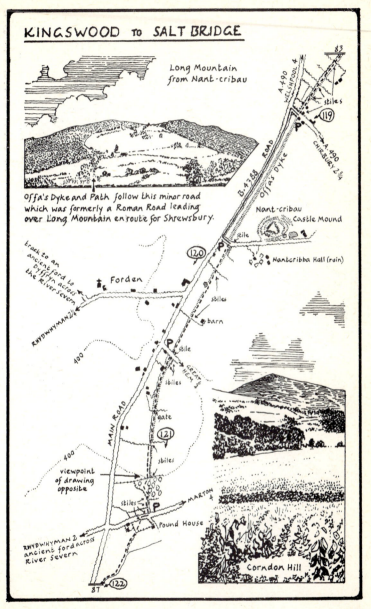

KINGSWOOD TO SALT BRIDGE

Long Mountain from Nant-cribau

Offa's Dyke and Path follow this minor road which was formerly a Roman Road leading over Long Mountain en route for Shrewsbury.

83

A.490 WELSHPOOL 4

stiles

119

A.490 CHIRBURY 2¾

B.4388 ROAD

Offa's Dyke

Nant-cribau Castle Mound

stile

Nantcribba Hall (ruin)

track to an ancient ford to Dyffryn across the River Severn

Forden

RHYDWHYMAN 2¼

120

stiles

barn

400

P stile

GREAT HEM ¾

stiles

MAIN ROAD

gate

121

sbiles

400

viewpoint of drawing opposite

stiles P

MARTON 4

RHYDWHYMAN 2 ancient ford across River Severn

Pound House

Corndon Hill

87 122

Montgomery from the point where Offa's Dyke crosses the Chirbury road.

CASTLE   FFRYDD FALDWYN (Hill Fort)

The town square of Montgomery (Trefaldwyn)

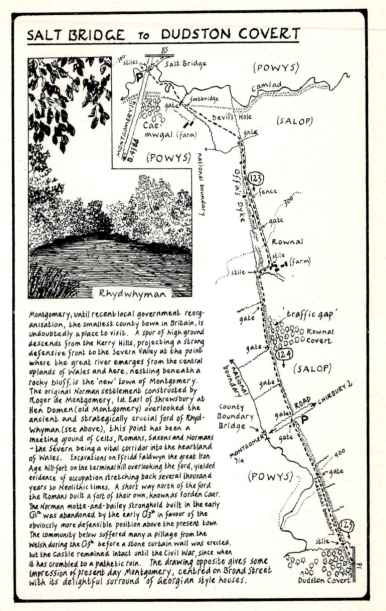

85
300' stiles
Salt Bridge
(POWYS)
P
Camlad
footbridge
gate
Devil's Hole
(SALOP)
Cae mwgal (farm)
gate
MONTGOMERY B.4368
(POWYS)
national boundary
Offa's Dyke
123
fence
700
gate
Rownal
stile (farm)
stile
gate
'traffic gap'
gate
Rownal covert
gate
124
NATIONAL BOUNDARY
(SALOP)
gate
ROAD
CHIRBURY 2
gate
County Boundary Bridge
P
MONTGOMERY 3/4
gate
400
gate
(POWYS)
NATIONAL BOUNDARY
125
stile
B4385
Dudston Covert

Rhydwhyman

Montgomery, until recent local government reorganisation, the smallest county town in Britain, is undoubtedly a place to visit. A spur of high ground descends from the Kerry Hills, projecting a strong defensive front to the Severn Valley at the point where the great river emerges from the central uplands of Wales and here, nestling beneath a rocky bluff, is the 'new' town of Montgomery. The original Norman settlement constructed by Roger de Montgomery, 1st. Earl of Shrewsbury at Hen Domen (old Montgomery) overlooked the ancient and strategically crucial ford of Rhyd-Whyman (see above), this point has been a meeting ground of Celts, Romans, Saxons and Normans – the Severn being a vital corridor into the heartland of Wales. Excavations on Ffridd Faldwyn the great Iron-Age hill-fort on the terminal hill overlooking the ford, yielded evidence of occupation stretching back several thousand years to Neolithic times. A short way north of the ford the Romans built a fort of their own, known as Forden Caer. The Norman motte-and-bailey stronghold built in the early C11th was abandoned by the early C13th in favour of the obviously more defensible position above the present town. The community below suffered many a pillage from the Welsh during the C13th before a stone curtain wall was erected, but the castle remained intact until the Civil War, since when it has crumbled to a pathetic ruin. The drawing opposite gives some impression of present day Montgomery, centred on Broad Street with its delightful surround of Georgian style houses.

Corndon Hill

Offa's Dyke at the Chirbury road crossing

Afon Camlad from Salt Bridge

OFFA'S DYKE

An excellently preserved section of Offa's Dyke heading south from the Chirbury road.

Two views of Offa's Dyke approaching Lack Brook, here defining the border.

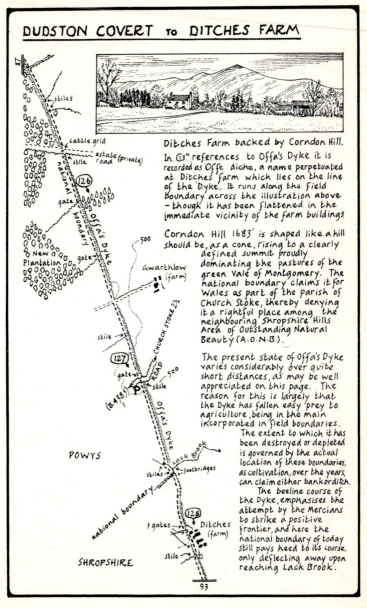

Ditches Farm backed by Corndon Hill.

In C13th references to Offa's Dyke it is recorded as Offe diche, a name perpetuated at Ditches farm which lies on the line of the Dyke. It runs along the field boundary across the illustration above - though it has been flattened in the immediate vicinity of the farm buildings.

Corndon Hill 1683' is shaped like a hill should be, as a cone, rising to a clearly defined summit proudly dominating the pastures of the green Vale of Montgomery. The national boundary claims it for Wales as part of the parish of Church Stoke, thereby denying it a rightful place among the neighbouring Shropshire Hills Area of Outstanding Natural Beauty (A.O.N.B.).

The present state of Offa's Dyke varies considerably over quite short distances, as may be well appreciated on this page. The reason for this is largely that the Dyke has fallen easy prey to agriculture, being in the main incorporated in field boundaries.
The extent to which it has been destroyed or depleted is governed by the actual location of these boundaries, as cultivation, over the years, can claim either bank or ditch.
The beeline course of the Dyke, emphasises the attempt by the Mercians to strike a positive frontier, and here the national boundary of today still pays heed to its course, only deflecting away upon reaching Lack Brook.

Map labels:
87
stiles
cattle grid
estate road (private)
stile
126
NATIONAL BOUNDARY
OFFA'S DYKE
gate
New Plantation
gate
500
Awarthlow (farm)
stile
ROAD CHURCH STOKE 2½
127
gate
500
stile
(B.478)
OFFA'S DYKE
POWYS
Lack Brook
stiles
footbridges
national boundary
3 gates
128
Ditches (farm)
stile
SHROPSHIRE
93

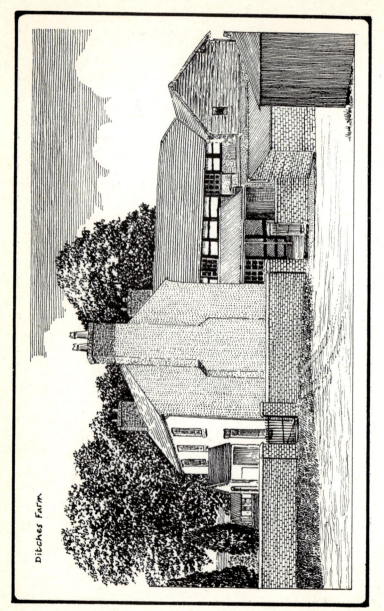

Ditches Farm

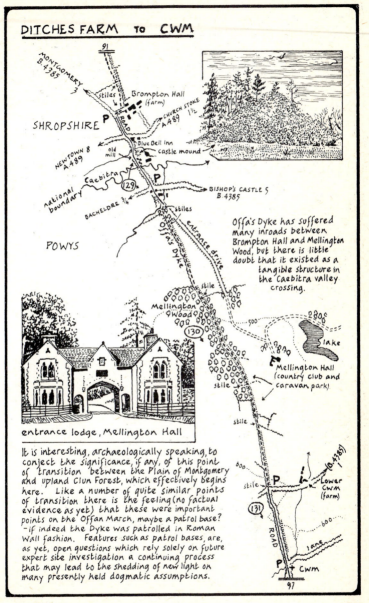

DITCHES FARM TO CWM

91

MONTGOMERY B.4385 3

stiles

Brompton Hall (farm)

CHURCH STOKE 1½

ROAD

A.489

SHROPSHIRE

P

Blue Bell Inn

NEWTOWN 8 A.489

old mill

castle mound

Caebitra

national boundary

129

P

BISHOP'S CASTLE 5 B.4385

BACHELDRE ¾

POWYS

stiles

Offa's Dyke

entrance drive

Offa's Dyke has suffered many inroads between Brompton Hall and Mellington Wood, but there is little doubt that it existed as a tangible structure in the Caebitra valley crossing.

stile

Mellington Wood

130

500

lake

stile

Mellington Hall (country club and caravan park)

stile

entrance lodge, Mellington Hall

It is interesting, archaeologically speaking, to conject the significance, if any, of this point of transition between the Plain of Montgomery and upland Clun Forest, which effectively begins here. Like a number of quite similar points of transition there is the feeling (no factual evidence as yet) that these were important points on the Offan March, maybe a patrol base? —if indeed the Dyke was patrolled in Roman Wall fashion. Features such as patrol bases are, as yet, open questions which rely solely on future expert site investigation a continuing process that may lead to the shedding of new light on many presently held dogmatic assumptions.

(B.4385)

stile

600

P

131

Lower Cwm (farm)

ROAD

600

lane

P

Cwm

97

93

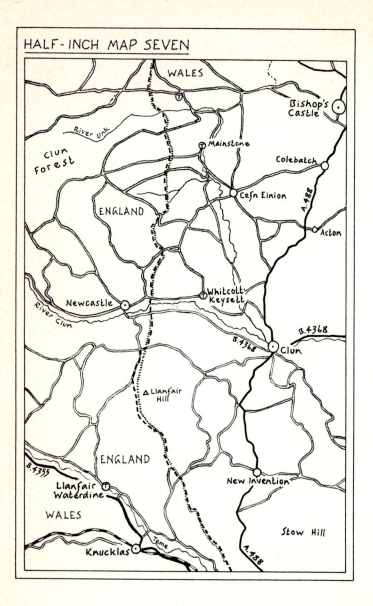

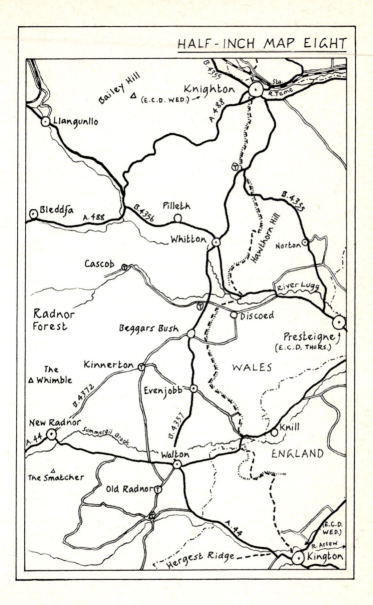

Offa's Dyke approaching the Kerry Hill Ridgeway

OFFA'S DYKE PATH

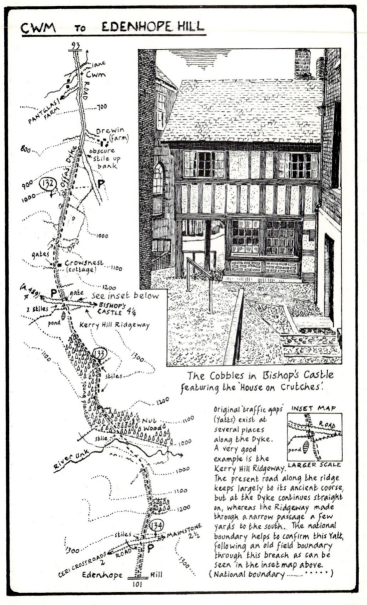

The Cobbles in Bishop's Castle featuring the 'House on Crutches'.

Map labels:
- 93
- lane
- Cwm
- ROAD
- PANTGLASIE FARM
- 700
- Drewin (farm)
- 800
- obscure stile up bank
- OFFA'S DYKE
- 900
- (132)
- 1000
- 1000
- gates
- Crowsnest (cottage)
- 1100
- 1200
- (A.489) x
- P
- gate
- see inset below
- BISHOP'S CASTLE 4¾
- 2 stiles
- pond
- Kerry Hill Ridgeway
- 1100
- (133)
- 1300
- stiles
- young plantation
- 1200
- Nut
- 1100
- Woods
- stile
- 1000
- River Unk
- 1000
- 1100
- 1200
- stiles
- (134)
- MAINSTONE 2½
- 1300
- P
- ROAD
- 1300
- CERI CROSSROADS 2
- Edenhope Hill
- 101

Original 'traffic gaps' (Yatts) exist at several places along the Dyke. A very good example is the Kerry Hill Ridgeway. The present road along the ridge keeps largely to its ancient course, but at the Dyke continues straight on, whereas the Ridgeway made through a narrow passage a few yards to the south. The national boundary helps to confirm this Yatt, following an old field boundary through this breach as can be seen in the inset map above. (National boundary ....•••••)

INSET MAP
- ROAD
- pond
- LARGER SCALE

Kerry Hill Ridgeway   Lan Fawr   Corndon Hill

Unk Valley

Offa's Dyke

View north from Edenhope Hill

Offa's Dyke   Edenhope Hill

View south along Offa's Dyke
and across the Unk Valley.

A rustic farm dwelling (occupied only by farm animals) at Churchtown.

View back down on alignment of Offa's Dyke to Churchtown, a community consisting two cottages and a simple church serving the parish of Mainstone.

99

Offa's Dyke crossing Edenhope Hill

Right-angle junction of Offa's Dyke
on the slopes of Hergan.

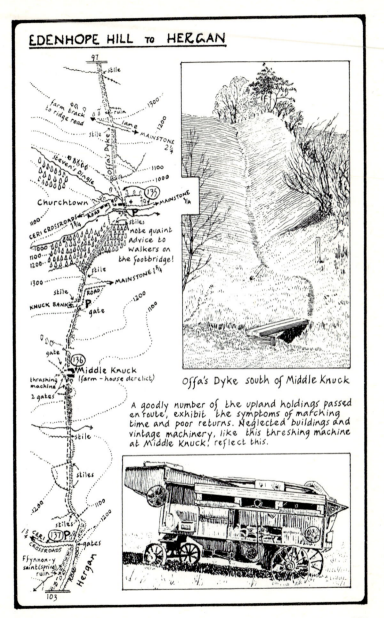

EDENHOPE HILL to HERGAN

97
stile

farm track
to ridge road

ruin
lane
MAINSTONE
2¼

1300
1200

Offa's Dyke

stile

Steven's Dingle

1100
1000

Churchtown

135

MAINSTONE
¼

CERI CROSSROADS
ROAD

stiles
note quaint
advice to
walkers on
the footbridge!

1100
1000
1100
1200

1300

stile

MAINSTONE 1¾

stile
KNUCK BANKS

P
gate

ROAD

1200
1100

gate

136
Middle Knuck
(farm-house derelict)

thrashing
machine

2 gates

stile

stiles

1200
1100
1200

stiles

136 CERI
CROSSROADS

137
P

2 gates

Ffynnon-y
saint (spring)
ruin

Hergan

103

Offa's Dyke south of Middle Knuck

A goodly number of the upland holdings passed
en route, exhibit the symptoms of matching
time and poor returns. Neglected buildings and
vintage machinery, like this threshing machine
at Middle Knuck, reflect this.

Offa's Dyke Path crossing the River Clun at Bryndrinog Farm.

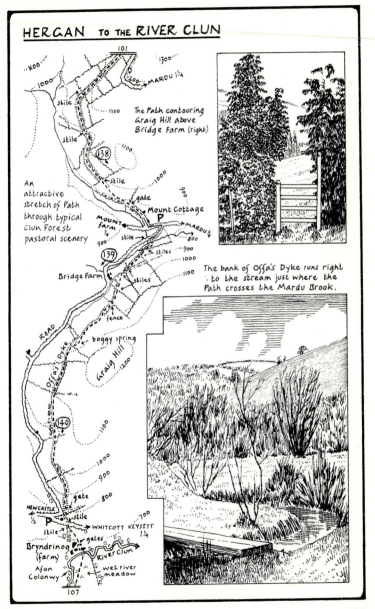

HERGAN TO THE RIVER CLUN

The Path contouring Graig Hill above Bridge Farm (right)

An attractive stretch of Path through typical Clun Forest pastoral scenery

The bank of Offa's Dyke runs right to the stream just where the Path crosses the Mardu Brook.

Map labels:
101
1400
1300
1000
1200
MARDU 1¼
stile
1100
stile
138
1100
1000
stile
gate
900
Mount Cottage
P
MOUNT farm ¼
900
stile
MARDU ½
800
139
stiles
900
1000
Bridge Farm
stiles
1100
fence
ROAD
Offa's Dyke
boggy spring
Graig Hill
1200
1100
140
1000
900
800
gate
NEWCASTLE ½
P
stile
700
stile
WHITCOTT KEYSETT 1¼
gates
Bryndrinog (farm)
River Clun
Afon Colonwy
wet river meadow
107

Church

Castle

Bridge

...the quietest place under the sun.....CLUN

View north from Offa's Dyke on Spoad Hill

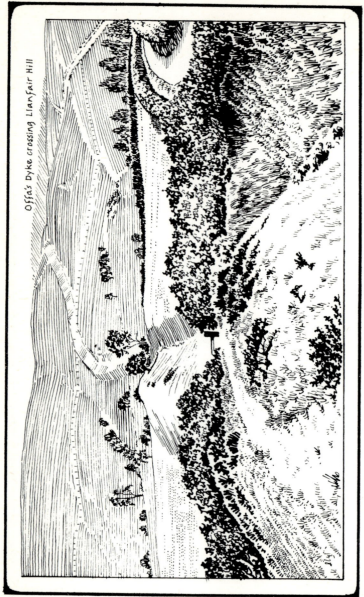

Offa's Dyke crossing Llanfair Hill

RIVER CLUN TO LLANFAIR HILL

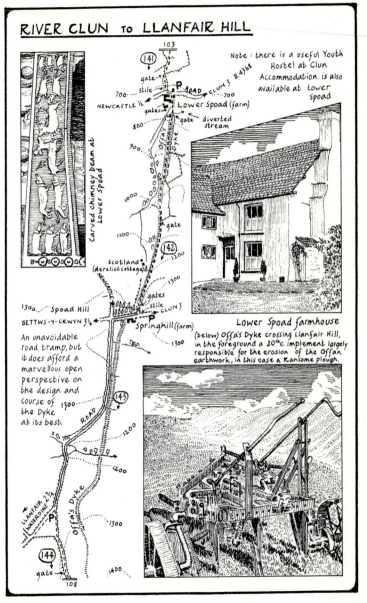

103

141

gate
stile

700

NEWCASTLE ½

800

900

1000

1100

1200

1300

Note: there is a useful Youth Hostel at Clun. Accommodation is also available at Lower Spoad

P ROAD   CLUN 3 B.4368

gates

Lower Spoad (farm)   700

gate   diverted stream

142

Scotland
(derelict cottage)

gates
stile   CLUN 3

Carved chimney beam at Lower Spoad

Lower Spoad farmhouse

(below) Offa's Dyke crossing Llanfair Hill, in the foreground a 20th c. implement largely responsible for the erosion of the Offan earthwork, in this case a Ransome plough.

1300   Spoad Hill
BETTWS-Y-CRWYN 3¼

An unavoidable road tramp, but it does afford a marvellous open perspective on the design and course of the Dyke at its best.

P   Springhill (farm)

1300

143

1300   ROAD

1200

1200

LLANFAIR 2¼
WATERDINE

P

Offa's Dyke

1300

144

gate

1400

108

LLANFAIR HILL TO THE SELLEY VALLEY

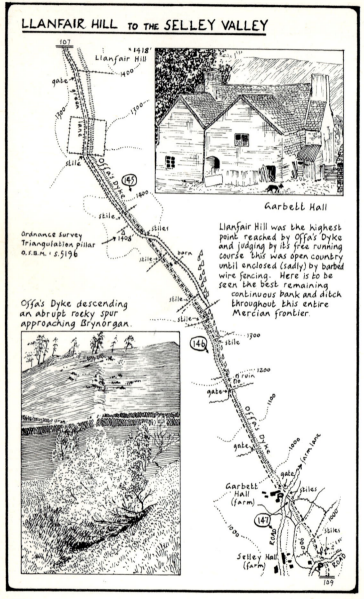

107

×1418'
Llanfair Hill
1400

gate

1300

1300

stile

Offa's Dyke

145

1400

stile

stiles

Ordnance Survey
Triangulation Pillar
O.S.B.M. : S.5196

△
1408

stile

barn

stile

stile

Garbett Hall

Llanfair Hill was the highest
point reached by Offa's Dyke
and judging by its free running
course this was open country
until enclosed (sadly) by barbed
wire fencing. Here is to be
seen the best remaining
continuous bank and ditch
throughout this entire
Mercian frontier.

Offa's Dyke descending
an abrupt rocky spur
approaching Brynorgan.

1300

146

stile

ruin

1200

gate

Offa's Dyke

1100

gate

1000

farm lane

gate

Garbett
Hall
(farm)

stiles

1000

147

ROAD

1000

Selley Hall
(farm)

1000

stiles

ROAD

109

108

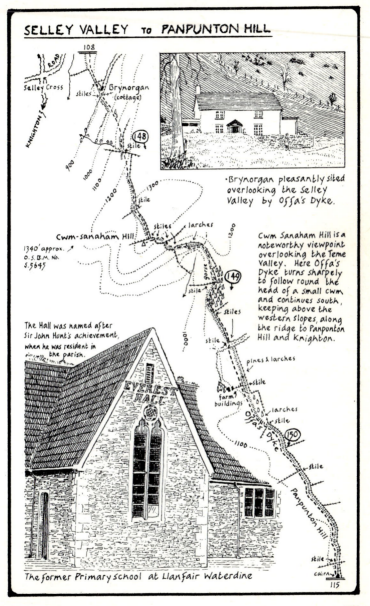

SELLEY VALLEY TO PANPUNTON HILL

108

Selley Cross

KNIGHTON ROAD

stiles · Brynorgan (cottage)

(148) stile

900 1000 1100 1200

1300 stile

Cwm-sanaham Hill

1340' approx.
O.S. B.M. No.
S.5645

stiles · larches

1200

stile gorse

(149)

stiles

1000'

stile

·Brynorgan pleasantly sited overlooking the Selley Valley by Offa's Dyke.

Cwm Sanaham Hill is a noteworthy viewpoint overlooking the Teme Valley. Here Offa's Dyke turns sharply to follow round the head of a small cwm and continues south, keeping above the western slopes, along the ridge to Panpunton Hill and Knighton.

The Hall was named after Sir John Hunt's achievement, when he was resident in the parish.

EVEREST HALL

pines & larches

stile

farm buildings

larches

stile

Offa's Dyke

(150)

1100

stile

Panpunton Hill

stile

cairn

115

The former Primary school at Llanfair Waterdine

109

The view from Cwm Sanahan Hill

The eight segments of view illustrated on the following three pages show the main portion of the panorama from Cwm Sanahan Hill. Offa's Dyke attains the highest point (now a junction of fences) near an Ordnance column and makes one of its few right angle bends. Presumably this was an agreed point to which the Dyke builders had to reach. The view itself is most rewarding, for here the first glimpse of the Black Mountains and Radnor Forest highlands are obtained to the south. Close at hand and very much the principal feature of the view is the Teme Valley with Knucklas directly below. Offa's Dyke is seen sweeping over Llanfair Hill to the north-west and continues in view along the ridge to Panpunton Hill where it descends out of sight to Knighton, rising again upon Ffridd to the south heading for Rhosymeirch.

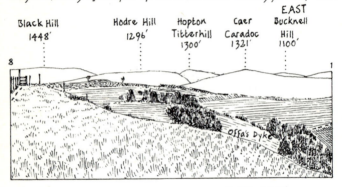

Black Hill	Hodre Hill	Hopton Titterhill	Caer Caradoc	EAST Bucknell Hill
1448'	1296'	1300'	1321'	1100'

8   1

Offa's Dyke

SOUTH-EAST

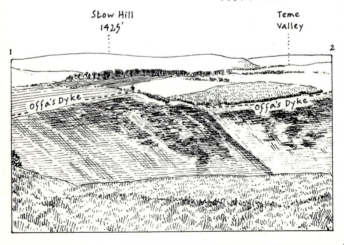

Stow Hill 1425'   Teme Valley

1   2

Offa's Dyke   Offa's Dyke

110

SOUTH

Panpunton Hill

Harley's Mountain 1265'

Knighton

Ffridd Hill

Garth Hill

River Teme

2

Offa's Dyke Path

Offa's Dyke

3

Black Mountains 22 miles

Rhos Hill 1283'

Bache Hill 2002'

Black Mixen 2135'

Radnor Forest 2166'

3

4

Knighton ← B.4355 → Newtown

River Teme

Skyborry Green

SOUTH-WEST

Fron-wen 1762'

Bailey Hill 1373'

Castle mound

Heyop

Cefn Coch

4

5

Knucklas

111

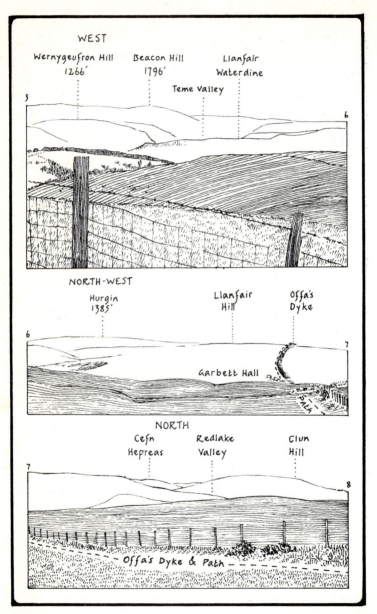

WEST

Wernygeufron Hill
1266'

Beacon Hill
1796'

Llanfair
Waterdine

Teme Valley

5

6

NORTH-WEST

Hurgin
1385'

Llanfair
Hill

Offa's
Dyke

6

Garbett Hall

PATH

7

NORTH

Cefn
Hepreas

Redlake
Valley

Clun
Hill

7

8

Offa's Dyke & Path

View back north on the ascent of Cwm Sanahan Hill to Garbett Hall and the high Dyke of Llanfair Hill

(above) Offa's Dyke Park
(below) Offa's Dyke Association and Mid-Wales Tourism Council Information Centre and projected Youth Hostel

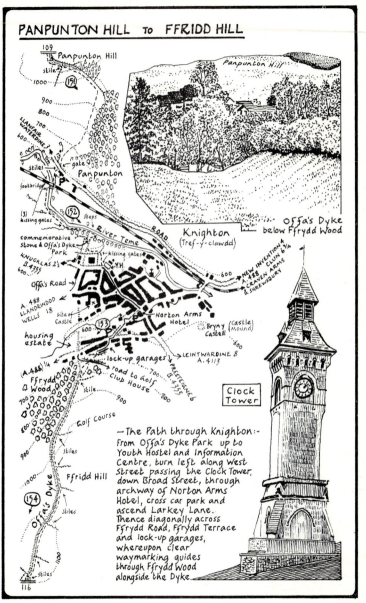

PANPUNTON HILL TO FFRIDD HILL

109 Panpunton Hill
stile
1000 · 151

900
800
700
LLANFAIR
WATERDINE?
600
stiles
gate
footbridge
Panpunton
Panpunton Hill
Offa's Dyke
below Ffridd Wood

(3) kissing gates
152 steps
River Teme
ROAD
Knighton
(Tref-y-clawdd)

commemorative
stone & Offa's Dyke
Park
KNUCKLAS 2½
B.4355
600
kissing gates
Y.H.

Offa's Road

A.488
LLANDRINDOD
WELLS 18
site of
Castle
600
153
Norton Arms
Hotel
Bryn y (castle)
Castell (mound)
600
NEW INVENTION
A.488 CLUN 6¾
CRAVEN ARMS
& SHREWSBURY

housing
estate

(A.488) ¼
Ffrydd
Wood
lock-up garages
road to Golf
Club House
stile
700
800
900
PRESTEIGNE 6
B.4355
LEINTWARDINE 8
A.4113

Golf Course
800
900
1000
Ffridd Hill
154
stiles
stiles

OFFA'S DYKE
1100
stiles
116

Clock
Tower

—The Path through Knighton:-
From Offa's Dyke Park up to
Youth Hostel and Information
Centre, turn left along West
Street passing the Clock Tower,
down Broad Street, through
archway of Norton Arms
Hotel, cross car park and
ascend Larkey Lane.
Thence diagonally across
Ffrydd Road, Ffrydd Terrace
and lock-up garages,
whereupon clear
waymarking guides
through Ffrydd Wood
alongside the Dyke.

115

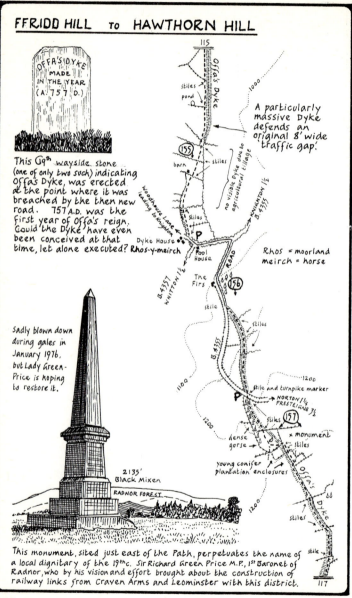

FFRIDD HILL TO HAWTHORN HILL

OFFA'S DYKE MADE IN THE YEAR (A. 757 D.)

This G9th wayside stone (one of only two such) indicating Offa's Dyke, was erected at the point where it was breached by the then new road. 757 A.D. was the first year of Offa's reign. Could the Dyke have even been conceived at that time, let alone executed? Rhos-y-meirch

Sadly blown down during gales in January 1976, but Lady Green-Price is hoping to restore it.

2135'
Black Mixen

RADNOR FOREST

This monument, sited just east of the Path, perpetuates the name of a local dignitary of the 19th c. Sir Richard Green Price M.P., 1st Baronet of Radnor, who by his vision and effort brought about the construction of railway links from Craven Arms and Leominster with this district.

115

Offa's Dyke

stiles
pond

155

barn
stiles

A particularly massive Dyke defends an original 8' wide 'traffic gap'.

no visible dyke due to agricultural tillage

KNIGHTON 1½ B.4355

Woodhouse Lane leading to Knighton

Stiles

P
Dyke House
Pool House

B.4357 WHITTON 1½

The Firs

stile

Rhos = moorland
meirch = horse

ROAD

156

stiles

B.4355

1200

stile and turnpike marker

NORTON 1¼
PRESTEIGNE 3½

157

stiles

dense gorse

× monument
stiles

young conifer plantation enclosures

Offa's Dyke

stiles

stile

117

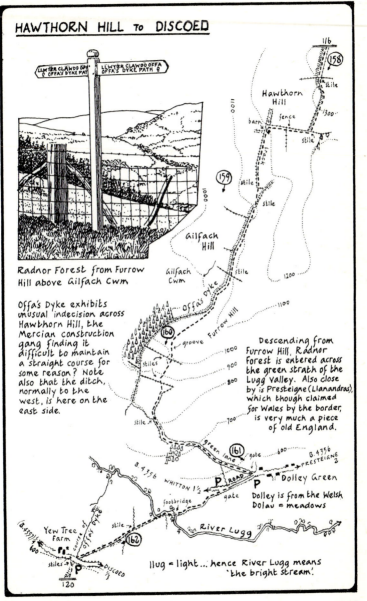

HAWTHORN HILL to DISCOED

LLWYBR CLAWDD OFFA & OFFA'S DYKE PATH

LLWYBR CLAWDD OFFA OFFA'S DYKE PATH

116

158

stile

Hawthorn Hill

1100

barn   fence

1300

stile

159

stile

stile

1200

Gilfach Hill

Gilfach Cwm

stile

Radnor Forest from Furrow Hill above Gilfach Cwm

Offa's Dyke

1100

Offa's Dyke exhibits unusual indecision across Hawthorn Hill, the Mercian construction gang finding it difficult to maintain a straight course for some reason? Note also that the ditch, normally to the west, is here on the east side.

160   groove Furrow Hill

1000

stiles

900

800

stile

700

Descending from Furrow Hill, Radnor Forest is entered across the green strath of the Lugg Valley. Also close by is Presteigne (Llanandras), which though claimed for Wales by the border, is very much a piece of old England.

green lane   161   gate   600   B.4356 PRESTEIGNE 2

B.4356

WHITTON 1½   P ROAD   P Dolley Green

footbridge   gate

Dolley is from the Welsh Dolau = meadows

Yew Tree Farm   stile   course of OFFA'S DYKE   River Lugg

600

162

stiles   P   DISCOED

120

llug = light ... hence River Lugg means 'the bright stream'.

The Radnorshire Arms Hotel at Presteigne

118

The Whimble 1965' and Black Mixen 2135' of Radnor Forest from the Dyke above Evenjobb Dingle - a delightful view across the Vale of Radnor.

View south from Barland Bank (Offa's Dyke) to Herrock Hill and Stanner Hill backed by the Hergest Ridge, to the left Offa's Dyke passes under Burfa Hill and is seen rising steeply onto Herrock Hill and contouring below the summit as a shelf ---

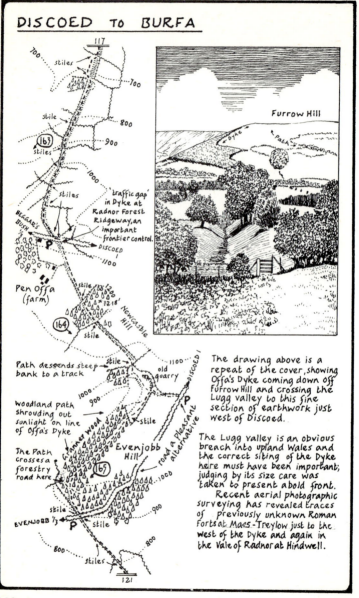

117

700

stiles

700

700

stile

800

163
stiles

900

1000

stiles

traffic gap' in Dyke at Radnor Forest Ridgeway, an important frontier control.

BEGGARS BUSH

DISCOED
1100

Pen Offa (farm)

stile

1200

1218'

Newcastle Hill

164

stile

Path descends steep bank to a track

stile

1100

old quarry

DISCOED

1000

900

Woodland path shrouding out sunlight on line of Offa's Dyke

stile

Granner Wood

Evenjobb Hill

165

road a pleasant alternative

The Path crosses a forestry road here

1000

stile

EVENJOBB ⅓

stile

P

900

stile

800

800

stiles

121

Furrow Hill

Path

The drawing above is a repeat of the cover, showing Offa's Dyke coming down off Furrow Hill and crossing the Lugg valley to this fine section of earthwork just west of Discoed.

The Lugg valley is an obvious breach into upland Wales and the correct siting of the Dyke here must have been important; judging by its size care was taken to present a bold front.

Recent aerial photographic surveying has revealed traces of previously unknown Roman Forts at Maes-Treylow just to the west of the Dyke and again in the Vale of Radnor at Hindwell.

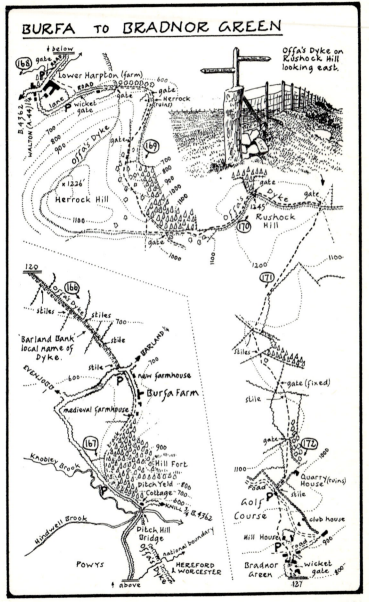

BURFA TO BRADNOR GREEN

Offa's Dyke on Rushock Hill looking east.

121

Ditch Hill Bridge spans the confluence of Hindwell and Knobley Brooks

Offa's Dyke crosses Rushock Hill on an unusual 'east-west' alignment, kinking to include the summit at 1245' (right-angle bend illustrated below), before descending to contour Herrock Hill (illustration opposite).

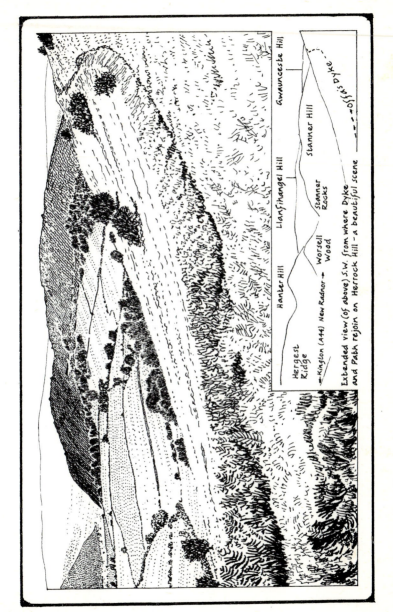

Hergest Ridge

← Kington (A44) New Radnor →   Worsell Wood

Hanter Hill   Llanfihangel Hill   Stanner Hill

Stanner Rocks

Gwauncester Hill

---- Offa's Dyke

Extended view (of above) S.W. from where Dyke and Path rejoin on Herrock Hill – a beautiful scene

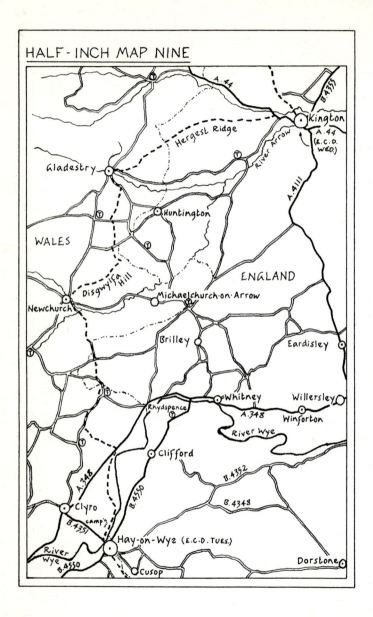

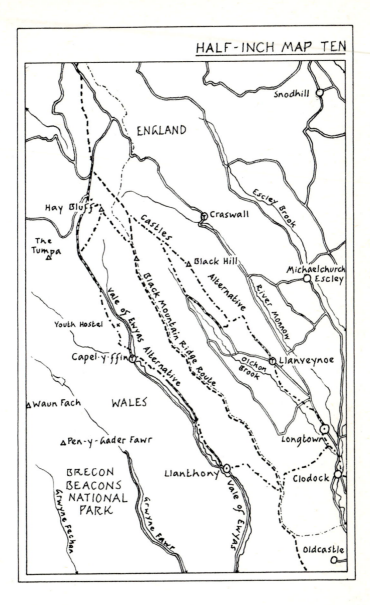

Snodhill

ENGLAND

Escley Brook

Hay Bluff

Castles

Craswall

The Tumpa

Black Hill

Michaelchurch Escley

Alternative

River Monnow

Vale of Ewyas Alternative

Black Mountain Ridge Route

Youth Hostel

Capel·y·ffin

Olchon Brook

Llanveynoe

△Waun Fach

WALES

△Pen·y·Gader Fawr

Longtown

BRECON BEACONS NATIONAL PARK

Llanthony

Vale of Ewyas

Clodock

Grwyne Fechan

Grwyne Fawr

Oldcastle

Hergest Croft

Footbridge and ford across Back Brook

BRADNOR GREEN to HERGEST CROFT

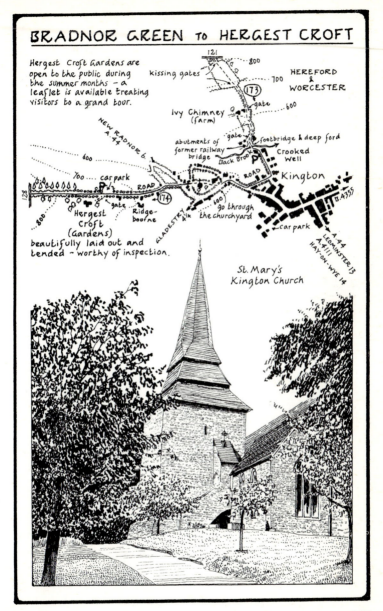

Hergest Croft Gardens are open to the public during the summer months — a leaflet is available treating visitors to a grand tour.

kissing gates

121
800
700
173
gate
600

HEREFORD & WORCESTER

Ivy Chimney (farm)

abutments of former railway bridge

gate

footbridge & deep ford

Back Brook

Crooked Well

NEW RADNOR 6. A.44

600

700   car park

ROAD

128

gate   Ridge-bourne

174

Hergest Croft (Gardens)

beautifully laid out and tended — worthy of inspection.

ROAD

Kington

B.4355

go through the churchyard

car park

GLADESTRY 4½

A.44
LEOMINSTER 13
A.4.11
HAY-ON-WYE 14

St. Mary's Kington Church

127

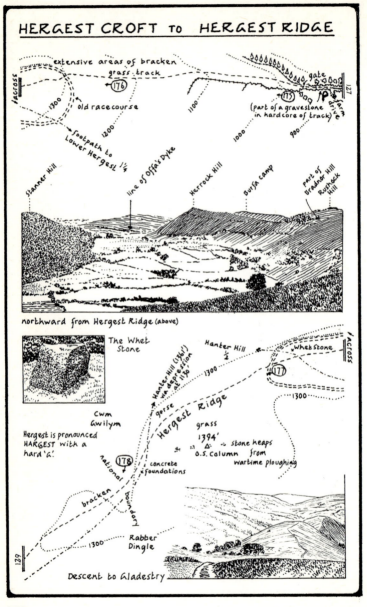

HERGEST CROFT to HERGEST RIDGE

extensive areas of bracken
grass track
(176)
old racecourse
1300
1200
footpath to
Lower Hergest 1¼

line of Offa's Dyke

gate

1100

(part of a gravestone
in hardcore of track)

1000

900

Stanner Hill

Herrock Hill

Burfa camp

part of
Bradnor Hill
Rushock
Hill

northward from Hergest Ridge (above)

The Whet
Stone

Hanter Hill (1361')
with depression
of 1130

Hanter Hill
½

Whet Stone

ACROSS

1300

(177)

1300

Cwm
Gwilym

gorse

Hergest Ridge

grass

1394'

△

O.S. Column

stone heaps
from
wartime ploughing

Hergest is pronounced
HARGEST with a
hard 'a'.

national boundary

(178)

concrete
foundations

bracken

1300

Rabber
Dingle

Descent to Gladestry

128

HERGEST RIDGE TO GROVE FARM

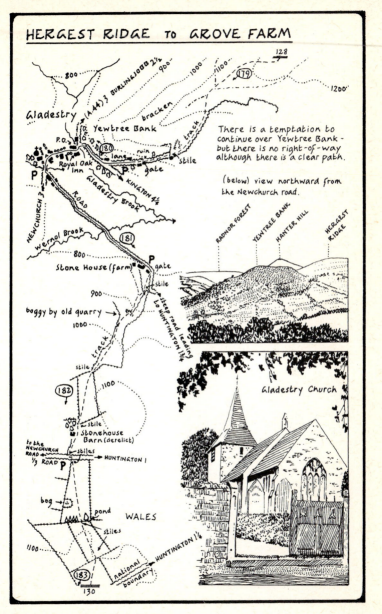

There is a temptation to continue over Yewtree Bank - but there is no right-of-way although there is a clear path.

(below) view northward from the Newchurch road.

Gladestry

Yewtree Bank

P.O.

Royal Oak Inn

Gladestry Brook

(A44) 3 BURLINGJOBB 2½

bracken

800

900

1000

1100

1200

128

179

track

ruin

gate

stile

lane

180

Gladestry Brook

KINGTON 4½

NEWCHURCH 3

ROAD

Wernol Brook

181

800

Stone House (farm)

gate

stile

900

baggy by old quarry

1000

track

steep road leading to HUNTINGTON 1¼

RADNOR FOREST   YEWTREE BANK   HANTER HILL   HERGEST RIDGE

stile

182

1100

stile

Stonehouse Barn (derelict)

to the NEWCHURCH ROAD

⅓ ROAD

stiles

HUNTINGTON 1

bog

pond

WALES

stiles

1100

HUNTINGTON 1½

national boundary

183

130

Gladestry Church

129

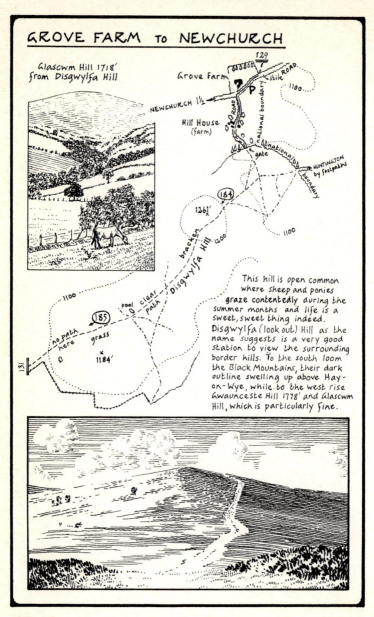

GROVE FARM TO NEWCHURCH

Glascwm Hill 1718'
from Disgwylfa Hill

129

Grove Farm

stile ROAD

NEWCHURCH 1½

1100

Hill House
(farm)

national boundary

gate

HUNTINGTON
by footpaths

national boundary

184

1261'
x

1100

bracken

Disgwylfa Hill

1200

1100

pool

clear path

185

no path
here

grass

131

x
1184'

This hill is open common
where sheep and ponies
graze contentedly during the
summer months and life is a
sweet, sweet thing indeed.
Disgwylfa (look out) Hill as the
name suggests is a very good
station to view the surrounding
border hills. To the south loom
the Black Mountains, their dark
outline swelling up above Hay-
on-Wye, while to the west rise
Gwaunceste Hill 1778' and Glascwm
Hill, which is particularly fine.

130

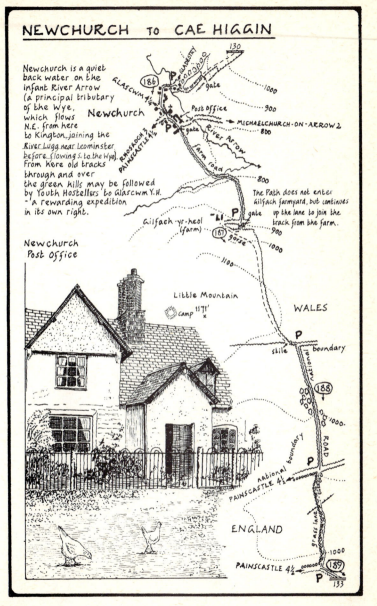

NEWCHURCH TO CAE HIGGIN

Newchurch is a quiet back water on the infant River Arrow (a principal tributary of the Wye, which flows N.E. from here to Kington, joining the River Lugg near Leominster before flowing S. to the Wye). From here old tracks through and over the green hills may be followed by Youth Hostellers to Glascwm Y.H. - a rewarding expedition in its own right.

GLADESTRY

GLASCWM 4½

186

gate

1000

900

Post office

Newchurch

MICHAELCHURCH-ON-ARROW 2

800

gate

River Arrow

RHOSADOCH 3
PAINSCASTLE 4½

farm road

800

The Path does not enter Gilfach farmyard, but continues up the lane to join the track from the farm.

Gilfach-yr-heol (farm)

gate

P

181

gorse

900

1000

Newchurch
Post Office

1100

Little Mountain

camp 1171'
×

WALES

P

stile

boundary

national

188

DDU ROAD

1000

P

national boundary

PAINSCASTLE 4½

ENGLAND

grass lane

1000

PAINSCASTLE 4½

189

P

133

131

The Rhydspence Inn stands right on the border with its back to the re-aligned A.438 road. In its former days it was a halting-place on an old drovers' route. A cider press in the carpark is a witness to the fact that it is just in Herefordshire, but no doubt the main attraction to Dyke Path wayfarers will be the cider inside!

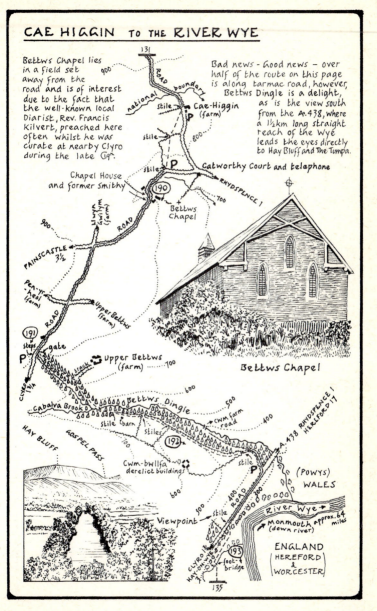

CAE HIGGIN TO THE RIVER WYE

Bettws Chapel lies in a field set away from the road and is of interest due to the fact that the well-known local Diarist, Rev. Francis Kilvert, preached here often whilst he was curate at nearby Clyro during the late C19th.

Chapel House and former smithy

Bad news - Good news - over half of the route on this page is along tarmac road, however, Bettws Dingle is a delight, as is the view south from the A.438, where a 1½km long straight reach of the Wye leads the eyes directly to Hay Bluff and The Tumpa.

131

ROAD

national boundary

900

stile

Cae-Higgin (farm)

P

stile

800

stile

P

Catworthy Court and telephone

190

RHYDSPENCE 1

700

Bettws Chapel

Llwyn (farm)

ROAD

900

PAINSCASTLE 3¼

Pen-yr-Aeol (farm)

ROAD

Upper Bettws (farm)

191

steps   gate

P

CLYRO 1½

Upper Bettws (farm) 700

Cabalva Brook

Bettws Dingle

600

600

500

stile   barn

stilers

192

Cwm farm road

400

A.438 RHYDSPENCE 1 HEREFORD 17

HAY BLUFF

GOSPEL PASS

Cwm-bwllfa derelict buildings

700

600

stile

P

(POWYS) WALES

500

ROAD

400

300

River Wye →

Monmouth approx. 64 miles (down river)

Viewpoint

stile

CLYRO 1½ HAY-ON-WYE 3¼

193

foot-bridge

ENGLAND (HEREFORD & WORCESTER)

135

Bettws Chapel

133

A few fragments remain of Hay's medieval town walls and Castle, illustrated here. The Castle houses the Antiquarian section of Richard Booth's second-hand book-shop.

RADNORSHIRE
→
COUNTY
ROADS.
Boundary
PARISH OF CLYRO
TO CLYRO 1
MILE.
and 75 yards

This milestone standing (1975) near the Wye bridge is worth preserving with the county now swallowed-up and metrication a sad new fact of life.

RIVER WYE to HAY-ON-WYE

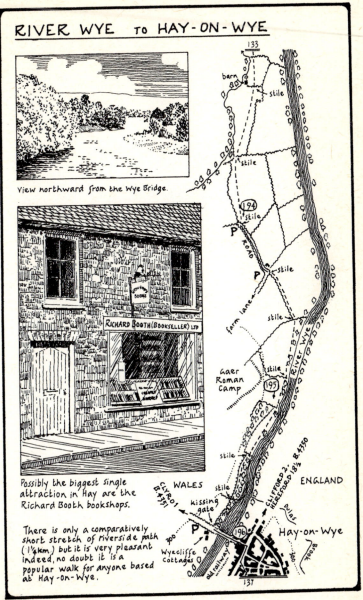

View northward from the Wye Bridge.

Possibly the biggest single attraction in Hay are the Richard Booth bookshops.

There is only a comparatively short stretch of riverside path (1¼ km) but it is very pleasant indeed, no doubt it is a popular walk for anyone based at Hay-on-Wye.

Map labels: 133, barn, stile, 194, stile, P, P ROAD, P, stile, farm lane, stile, Gaer Roman Camp, stile, 195, River Wye, B-4-350, CLIFFORD 2. HEREFORD 18¼. B4350, stile, stile, WALES, ENGLAND, CLYRO 1. B.4351, kissing gate, stile, P, 196, Hay-on-Wye, Wyecliffe Cottages, old railway, Dulas Brook, 137

RICHARD BOOTH (BOOKSELLER) LTD

BOOKS

Hay Bluff (Pen-y-Beacon) from the head of the Dulas Valley on the road from Hay-on-Wye to Craswall.

HAY-ON-WYE TO CADWGAN

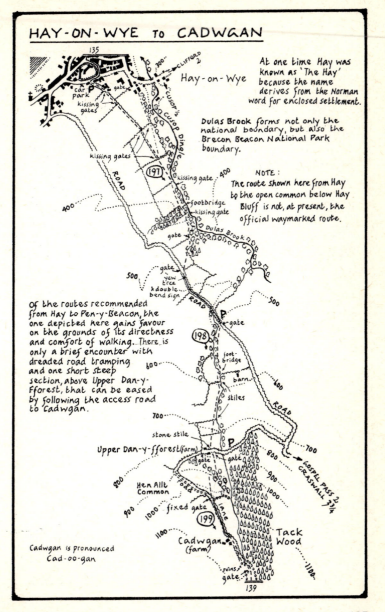

At one time Hay was known as 'The Hay' because the name derives from the Norman word for enclosed settlement.

Dulas Brook forms not only the national boundary, but also the Brecon Beacon National Park boundary.

NOTE :
The route shown here from Hay to the open common below Hay Bluff is not, at present, the official waymarked route.

Of the routes recommended from Hay to Pen-y-Beacon, the one depicted here gains favour on the grounds of its directness and comfort of walking. There is only a brief encounter with dreaded road tramping and one short steep section, above Upper Dan-y-Fforest, that can be eased by following the access road to Cadwgan.

Cadwgan is pronounced Cad-oo-gan

Hay-on-Wye

CLIFFORD 2

car park

kissing gates

kissing gates

ROAD

191

kissing gate

footbridge

kissing gate

gate

Dulas Brook

gate
yew tree
double bend sign

ROAD

500

500

P

198

footbridge

barn

stiles

ROAD

600

600

stone stile

Upper Dan-y-fforest (farm)

P

gate

gate

GOSPEL PASS 2 / CRASWALL 3¼

700

800

700

Hen Allt Common

ROAD

900

1000

fixed gate

LANE

199

Cadwgan (farm)

Tack Wood

ruins
gate

1100

1100

135

400

400

400

500

600

700

800

900

1000

900

1000

1100

139

197

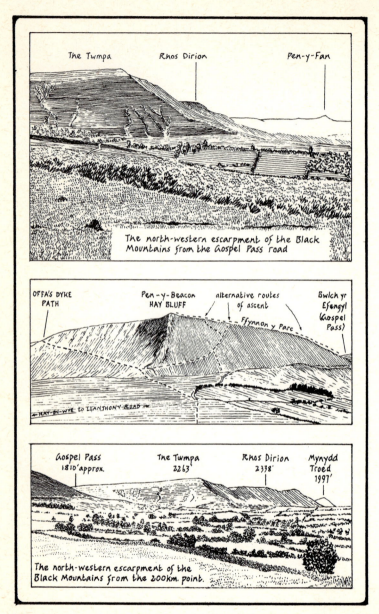

The Twmpa   Rhos Dirion   Pen-y-Fan

The north-western escarpment of the Black Mountains from the Gospel Pass road

OFFA'S DYKE PATH   Pen-y-Beacon HAY BLUFF   alternative routes of ascent   Bwlch yr Efengyl (Gospel Pass)

Ffynnon y Parc

← HAY-ON-WYE to LLANTHONY ROAD →

Gospel Pass 1810' approx.   The Twmpa 2263'   Rhos Dirion 2338'   Mynydd Troed 1997'

The north-western escarpment of the Black Mountains from the 200km. point.

CADWGAN TO HAY BLUFF

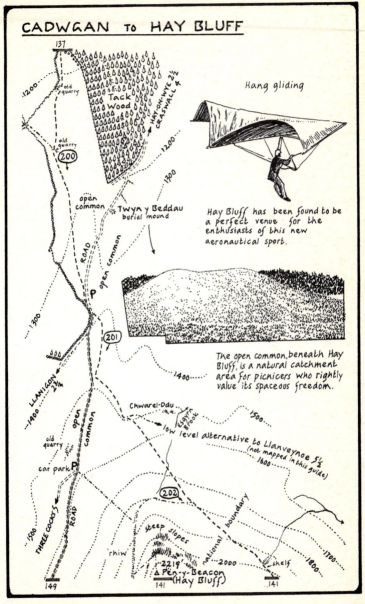

137

old quarry

1200

Tack Wood

HAY ON WYE 2½ CRASWALL 4

200

old quarry

1200

1300

open common

ROAD

Twyn y Beddau
burial mound

open common

1300

201

LLANIGON 2¼

1400

open common

old quarry

car park P

THREE COCKS

ROAD

1500

Chwarel-Ddu

Escyfn Brook

1400

1500

low level alternative to Llanveynoe 5½
(not mapped in this guide)

1600

202

steep slopes

national boundary

1700

rhiw

2219
△ Pen-y-Beacon
(Hay Bluff)

2000

shelf

1800

149

141

141

.141

Hang gliding

Hay Bluff has been found to be a perfect venue for the enthusiasts of this new aeronautical sport.

The open common, beneath Hay Bluff, is a natural catchment area for picnicers who rightly value its spacious freedom.

WYE VALLEY BELOW   TACK WOOD

OFFA'S DYKE PATH ASCENDING FROM HAY   GOSPEL PASS ROAD FROM HAY →

OPEN COMMON

The Path rises from the broad common (under the great prow of Hay Bluff),
on a rhiw track that develops into a groove (top sketch), rising
further to a shelf, at a pronounced corner. At which point shallow
gullies descend (bottom sketch), this is the source of the Afon Mynwy (River
Monnow). Discriminating walkers may like to leave the official long-
distance route and follow the Castles Alternative, which effectively
begins here – refer to pages 155-160 and 179-186 – thereby enjoying a
beautiful river valley from its source to confluence with the Wye at Monmouth.

The Monnow Valley   Black Hill   Crib y Garth

140

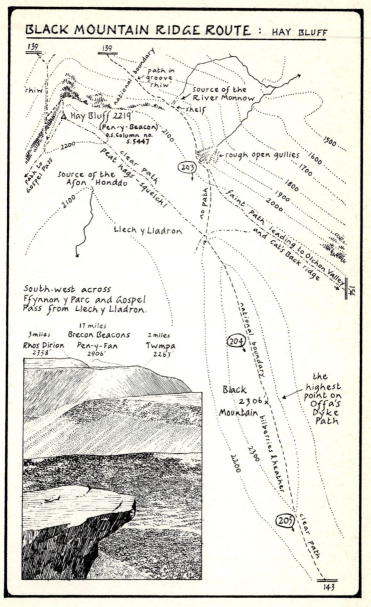

BLACK MOUNTAIN RIDGE ROUTE : HAY BLUFF

139

139

rhiw

path in groove
'rhiw'

national boundary

source of the
River Monnow

shelf

△ Hay Bluff 2219'
(Pen-y-Beacon)
O.S. column no.
S.5447

2100

2200

clear Path

Peat hags — squelch!

rough open gullies

203

1500

1600

1700

1800

1900

2000

path to
Gospel Pass

source of the
Afon Honddu

2100

Llech y Lladron

no path

faint path leading to Olchon Valley
and Cat's Back ridge

154

South-west across
Ffynnon y Parc and Gospel
Pass from Llech y Lladron.

17 miles
Brecon Beacons

3 miles   2 miles
Rhos Dirion   Pen-y-Fan   Twmpa
2338'   2906'   2263'

national boundary

204

Black
Mountain
2306 x

the
highest
point on
Offa's
Dyke
Path

bilberries & heather

2300

2200

clear path

205

143

141

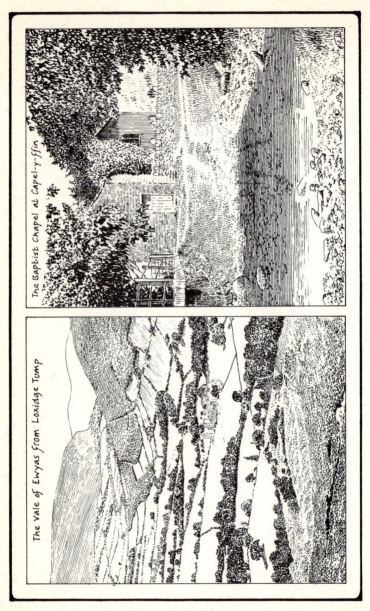

The Vale of Ewyas from Loxidge Tump

The Baptist Chapel at Capel-y-ffin

142

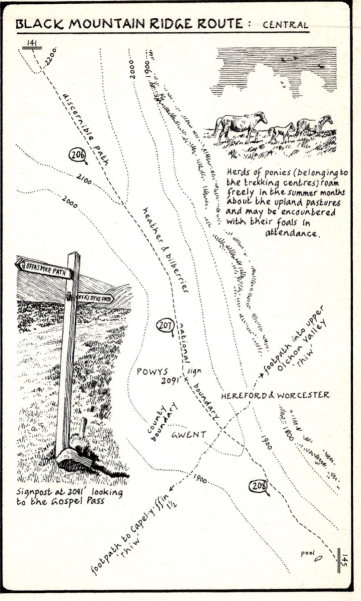

141

2200

discernible path

206

2100

2000

2000

1900

heather & bilberries

Herds of ponies (belonging to the trekking centres) roam freely in the summer months about the upland pastures and may be encountered with their foals in attendance.

OFFA'S DYKE PATH

OFFA'S DYKE PATH

207

national sign

POWYS
2091'

footpath into upper Olchon Valley 'rhiw'

county boundary

HEREFORD & WORCESTER

GWENT

1800

1900

208

Signpost at 2091' looking to the Gospel Pass

1900

footpath to Capel-y-ffin 'rhiw' 1½

pool

145

143

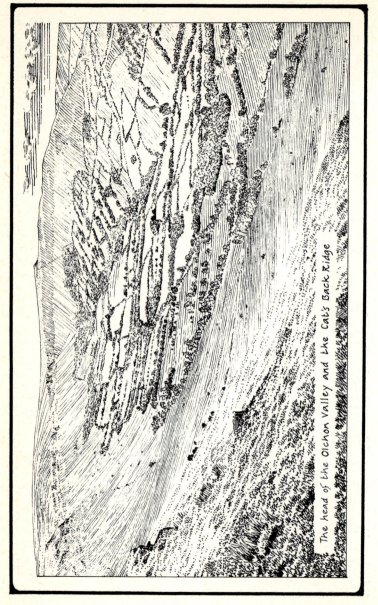

The head of the Olchon Valley and the Cat's Back Ridge

BLACK MOUNTAIN RIDGE ROUTE : RED DAREN

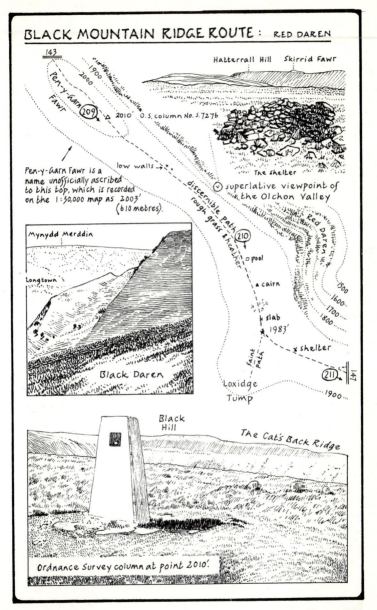

143

Pen-y-barn Fawr

2000

1900

209 △ 2010 O.S. column No. S.7276

Hatterrall Hill   Skirrid Fawr

The shelter

Pen-y-barn Fawr is a name unofficially ascribed to this top, which is recorded on the 1:50,000 map as 2003' (610 metres).

low walls →

⊙ superlative viewpoint of the Olchon Valley

discernible path

rough grass & heather

Red Daren

210

○ pool

▲ cairn

✗ slab
1983'

1500

1600

1700

1800

✗ shelter

211

147

faint path

Loxidge Tump

1900

Mynydd Merddin

Longtown

Black Daren

Black Hill

The Cat's Back Ridge

Ordnance Survey column at point 2010'.

145

Two views of Llanthony,
an Augustine Priory which
was completed in 1115 A.D.,
but local hostility caused
the monks to quit the place
finding safer quarters at
Gloucester. The romance
and magnificence of the
place today is heightened
by the setting of the ruins,
tranquil amid a green vale
with steep bracken slopes
rising at every hand - its
popularity is justified.

BLACK MOUNTAIN RIDGE ROUTE: BLACK DAREN and LLANTHONY

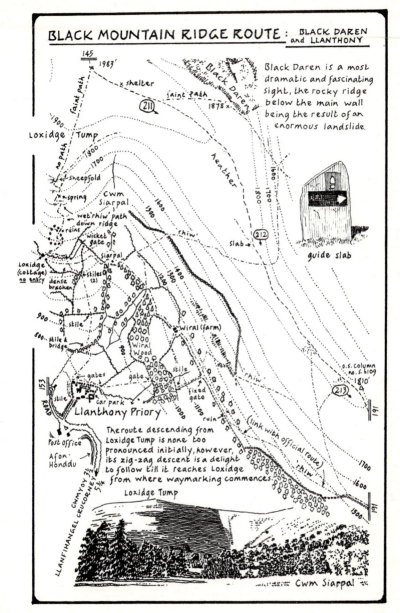

Black Daren is a most dramatic and fascinating sight, the rocky ridge below the main wall being the result of an enormous landslide.

145 1983'
× shelter
faint path
211
faint path
1878 ×
Loxidge Tump
no path
1900
1800
1700
heather
1800
1700
1600
× sheepfold
spring
Cwm Siarpal
'rhiw'
1500
1500
wet 'rhiw' path down ridge
ruins
wicket gate
Siarpal
slab
212
guide slab

Loxidge (cottage) no entry
stiles (2)
dense bracken
1400
1500
1400

900
stile
Wiral (farm)
800
stile & bridge
Wiral Wood
'rhiw'
o.s. column no. S.6109
1810'
213
191

gates
gate
stile
stile
car park
fixed gate
Llanthony Priory
ruin
(link with official route)
'rhiw'
1700
1600
1500
191

153 ROAD

Post Office
Afon Honddu

The route descending from Loxidge Tump is none too pronounced initially, however, its zig-zag descent is a delight to follow till it reaches Loxidge from where waymarking commences.

LLANFIHANGEL CRUCORNEY 5¼
LLANFIHANGEL CRUCORNEY 3½

Loxidge Tump

Cwm Siarpal

147

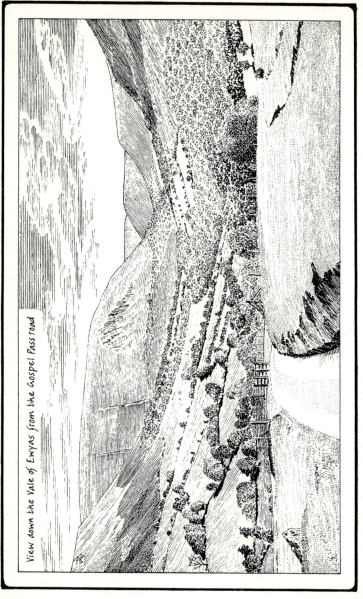

View down the Vale of Ewyas from the Gospel Pass road

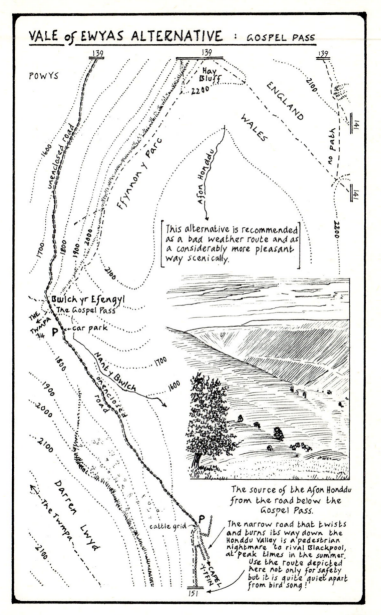

VALE of EWYAS ALTERNATIVE : GOSPEL PASS

POWYS

ENGLAND

WALES

Hay Bluff
2200

Ffynnon y Parc

Afon Honddu

no path

> This alternative is recommended as a bad weather route and as a considerably more pleasant way scenically.

Bwlch yr Efengyl
The Gospel Pass
THE TWMPA ¼
P car park

Nant y Bwlch
Unenclosed road

Darren Lwyd
The Twmpa

cattle grid
P

CAPEL-Y-FFIN

151

The source of the Afon Honddu from the road below the Gospel Pass.

The narrow road that twists and turns its way down the Honddu Valley is a pedestrian nightmare to rival Blackpool at peak times in the summer. Use the route depicted here not only for safety but it is quite quiet apart from bird song !

The Castle, Youth Hostel

KING GEORGE VI
MEMORIAL YOUTH HOSTEL
CAPEL-Y-FFIN

Church of England chapel
at Capel-y-ffin

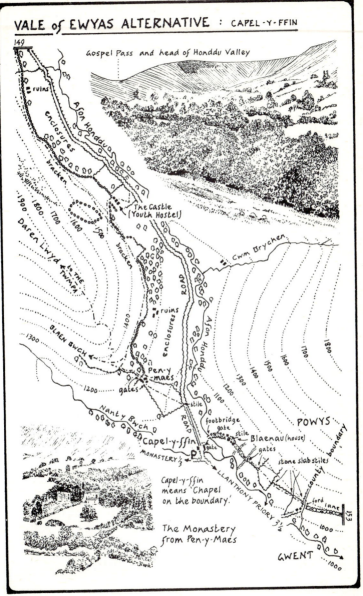

VALE of EWYAS ALTERNATIVE : CAPEL-Y-FFIN

149

Gospel Pass and head of Honddu Valley

ruins

enclosures

Afon Honddu

bracken

1900 1800 1700 1600 1500

Daren Lwyd

to THE TWMPA

The Castle
(Youth Hostel)

Cwm Brychen

ROAD

bracken

1400

ruins

enclosures

Afon Honddu

1800 1700 1600 1500 1400 1300

1300

GLAEN BWCH

Pen-y-maes

1200 gates

1200 1100

Nant y Bwch

stile

Road

footbridge
gate

POWYS

Capel-y-ffin

MONASTERY ½

P

gate

stile

Blaenau (house)

gates

stone slab stiles

county boundary

Capel-y-ffin
means 'Chapel
on the boundary.'

LLANTHONY PRIORY 3½

ford lane

153

The Monastery
from Pen-y-Maes

1000

GWENT

1000

151

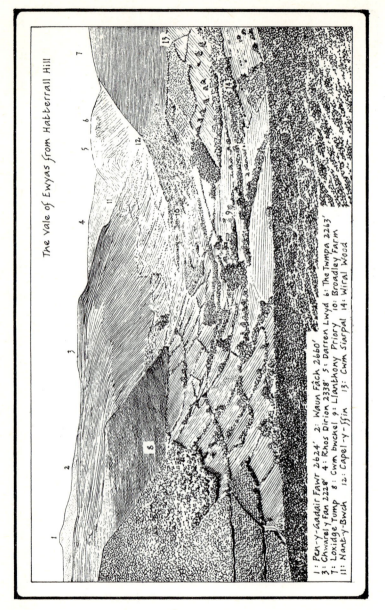

The Vale of Ewyas from Hatterrall Hill

1: Pen-y-Gaddir Fawr 2624' 2: Waun Fâch 2660'
3: Chwarel y Fan 2228' 4: Rhos Dirion 2338' 5: Darren Lwyd 6: The Twmpa 2263'
7: Loxidge Tump 8: Cwm bwchel 9: Llanthony Priory 10: Broadley Farm
11: Nant-y-Bwch 12: Capel-y-ffin 13: Cwm Siarpal 14: Wiral Wood

152

VALE of EWYAS ALTERNATIVE : TAFOLOG

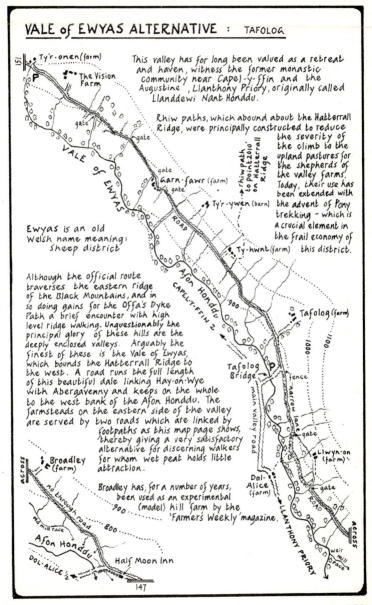

This valley has for long been valued as a retreat and haven, witness the former monastic community near Capel-y-ffin and the Augustine, Llanthony Priory, originally called Llanddewi Nant Honddu.

Rhiw paths, which abound about the Hatterrall Ridge, were principally constructed to reduce the severity of the climb to the upland pastures for the shepherds of the valley farms. Today, their use has been extended with the advent of Pony trekking - which is a crucial element in the frail economy of this district.

Ewyas is an old Welsh name meaning: sheep district

Although the official route traverses the eastern ridge of the Black Mountains, and in so doing gains for the Offa's Dyke Path a brief encounter with high level ridge walking. Unquestionably the principal glory of these hills are the deeply enclosed valleys. Arguably the finest of these is the Vale of Ewyas, which bounds the Hatterrall Ridge to the west. A road runs the full length of this beautiful dale linking Hay-on-Wye with Abergavenny and keeps on the whole to the west bank of the Afon Honddu. The farmsteads on the eastern side of the valley are served by two roads which are linked by footpaths as this map page shows, thereby giving a very satisfactory alternative for discerning walkers for whom wet peat holds little attraction.

Broadley has, for a number of years, been used as an experimental (model) hill farm by the 'Farmers Weekly' magazine.

Map labels: Ty'r-onen (farm); 151; The Vision Farm; P; gate; gate; VALE of EWYAS; gate; Garn-fawr (farm); gate; gate; rhiw path to point 2010 on Hatterrall Ridge; Ty'r-ywen (barn); ROAD; Afon Honddu; Ty-hwnt (farm); CAPEL-Y-FFIN 2; 900; Tafolog (farm); 1100; Tafolog Bridge; 1000; fence; main valley road; narrow lane; gate; Llwyn-on (farm); Dol-Alice (farm); gate; Broadley (farm); across; no through road; old mill race; 900; 800; LLANTHONY PRIORY; across; weir; mill race; Afon Honddu; DOL-ALICE ½; Half Moon Inn

147

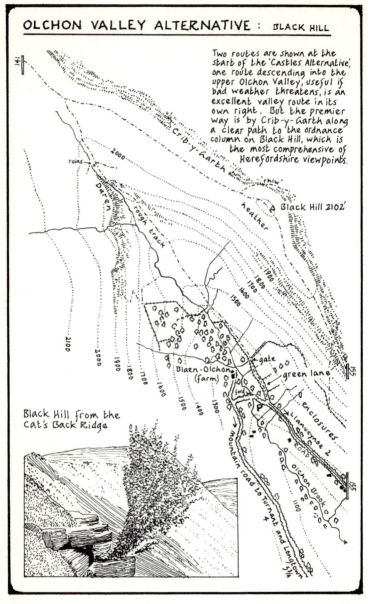

Two routes are shown at the start of the 'Castles Alternative', one route descending into the upper Olchon Valley, useful if bad weather threatens, is an excellent valley route in its own right. But the premier way is by Crib-y-Garth along a clear path to the ordnance column on Black Hill, which is the most comprehensive of Herefordshire viewpoints.

141

Crib-y-Garth

rhiw

△ Black Hill 2102'

2000

ruins →

Daren

rough track

heather

2100

2000

1900

1800

1700

1600

1500

1400

1300

1900

1800

1700

1600

1500

gate

Blaen-Olchon (farm)

green lane

ford

P

enclosures

Llanveynoe 2

155

Olchon Brook

1300
1200
1100

mountain road to Turnant and Longtown 5¾

Black Hill from the Cat's Back Ridge

154

OLCHON VALLEY ALTERNATIVE : CAT'S BACK

small quarries

Cat's Back Ridge

154

ROAD

enclosures

bracken

154

track to Craswall

track to Craswall

Should you be seeking one border country walk, not necessarily in the company of the Mercian frontier mark, but with far ranging border landscapes as a must – then park your car at the picnic area indicated below and follow the 6½ mile (10km) circular walk shown on these two pages. This most rewarding excursion climbs directly up to the narrow crest of the unusually named and unique rocky top of the Cat's Back Ridge and continues to Black Hill and Crib-y-Garth returning by Daren on a track descending into the Olchon Valley, completing the circuit along the Llanveynoe road.

stile
car park & picnic area
gate
fence
gates
stile
gate

The Cat's Back is different, indeed it should hold a special place for Herefordians as a point of unrivalled breadth of view out across ridges into the misty plain of distance. This is something to be enjoyed at a more leisurely pace – not rushed over.

LLANVEYNOE LONGTOWN 4

1293
Little Black Hill

gates

Blackhill Farm

ROAD

156

The rocky crest of the exciting Cat's Back Ridge

155

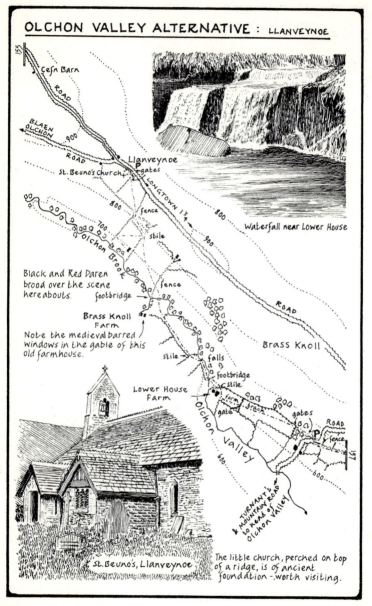

OLCHON VALLEY ALTERNATIVE : LLANVEYNOE

155

Cefn Barn

ROAD

BLAEN OLCHON

900

ROAD

Llanveynoe

gates

St. Beuno's church

LONGTOWN 13¾

800

800

fence

Olchon Brook

700

stile

900

Black and Red Daren
brood over the scene
hereabouts.

fence

footbridge

ROAD

Brass Knoll
Farm

Brass Knoll

Note the medieval barred
windows in the gable of this
old farmhouse.

stile

falls

footbridge

stile

Lower House
Farm

farm brace

Olchon Valley

gate

gates

ROAD

P

fence

157

600

600

TURNANT'S
MOUNTAIN ROAD
to head of
Olchon Valley

Waterfall near Lower House

St. Beuno's, Llanveynoe

The little church, perched on top
of a ridge, is of ancient
foundation - worth visiting.

OLCHON VALLEY ALTERNATIVE : LONGTOWN

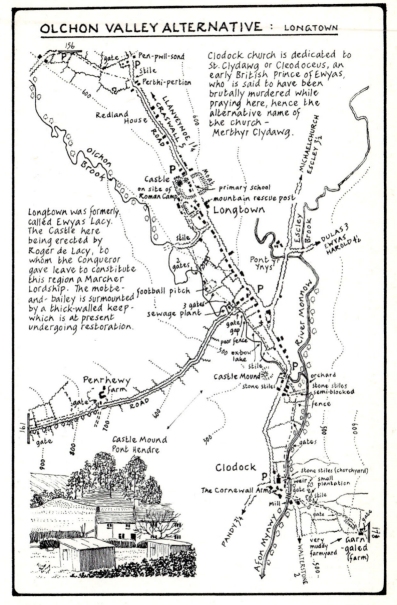

156

gate · Pen-pwll-sond
P
Stile
Perthi-pertion

Redland House

600

600

LLANVEYNOE 1¼
CRASWALL 5
ROAD

Olchon Brook

Clodock church is dedicated to St. Clydawg or Cleodoceus, an early British prince of Ewyas, who is said to have been brutally murdered while praying here, hence the alternative name of the church – Merthyr Clydawg.

MICHAELCHURCH ESCLEY 3½

P
Castle
on site of Roman Camp

primary school
mountain rescue post
Longtown

stile

Longtown was formerly called Ewyas Lacy. The Castle here being erected by Roger de Lacy, to whom the Conqueror gave leave to constitute this region a Marcher Lordship. The motte-and-bailey is surmounted by a thick-walled keep which is at present undergoing restoration.

2 gates

football pitch

3 gates
sewage plant

gate/gap
poor fence

500 ex-bow lake

Pont yr Ynys

P

Escley
Escley Brook

DULAS 3
EWYAS HAROLD 4½

River Monnow

stile

Castle Mound
stone stiles

P
orchard
stone stiles
semi-blocked
fence

Penrhewy farm

gate
ROAD
700
800
600

161

gate

Castle Mound
Pont Hendre

500

gates

600
600

Clodock

P
The Cornewall Arms

stone stiles (churchyard)
small plantation
weir
gate
mill
stile

PANDY 3¼

gate

very muddy farmyard

WALTERSTONE

500

Afon Mynwy

garn-galed (farm)

148

over saddle to
LLANTHONY PRIORY

HATTERRALL HILL ← → HAY BLUFF

← LINK PATH TO LONGTOWN

Garn-galed Farm looking to
the high Hatterrall Hill ridge

Longtown Church

1 : Longtown Castle
2 : Primary School
3 : Olchon Valley
4 : Cat's Back Ridge
5 : Black Hill
6 : Earthworks of
    Roman Fort or Camp

Longtown

158

Black Daren   Red Daren   Olchon Valley   Cat's Back Ridge

Black Hill

The ancient church of St. Clydawg at Clodock contains many notable features including a minstrels' gallery and a churchyard with a very large number of memorial stones.

The view above gives some idea of its setting at the foot of the dark high mass of the Hatterrall Hill ridge. (An excellent pamphlet guide is available within the church).

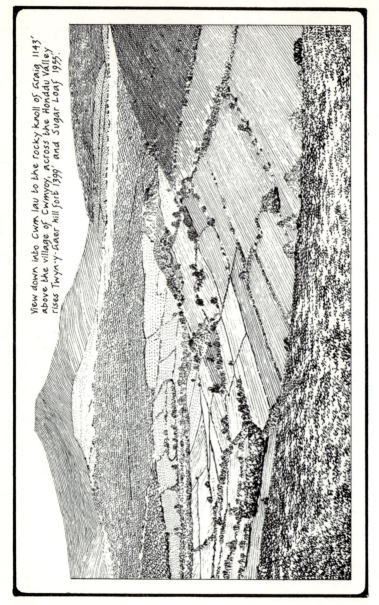

View down into Cwm Iau to the rocky knoll of Graig 1143'
above the village of Cwmyoy, across the Honddu Valley
rises Twyn-y-Gaer hill fort 1399' and Sugar Loaf 1955'.

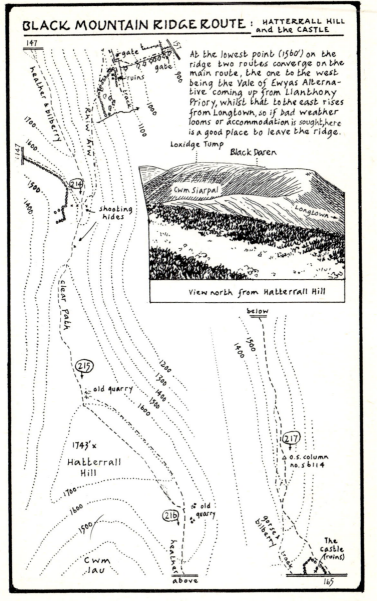

BLACK MOUNTAIN RIDGE ROUTE : HATTERRALL HILL and the CASTLE

At the lowest point (1560') on the ridge two routes converge on the main route, the one to the west being the Vale of Ewyas Alternative coming up from Llanthony Priory, whilst that to the east rises from Longtown, so if bad weather looms or accommodation is sought, here is a good place to leave the ridge.

147

gate

gate

ruins

157

900

1000

1100

track

track

Railway

heather & bilberry

1700

147

1600

1500

1400

214

shooting hides

clear path

Loxidge Tump

Black Daren

Cwm Siarpal

Longtown →

View north from Hatterrall Hill

below

1500

1400

215

old quarry

1200

1300

1400

1500

1600

217

△ o.s. column no. s 6114

1743' x

Hatterrall Hill

1700

1600

1500

216

old quarry

heather

above

Cwm Iau

gorse & bilberry

track

The Castle (ruins)

165

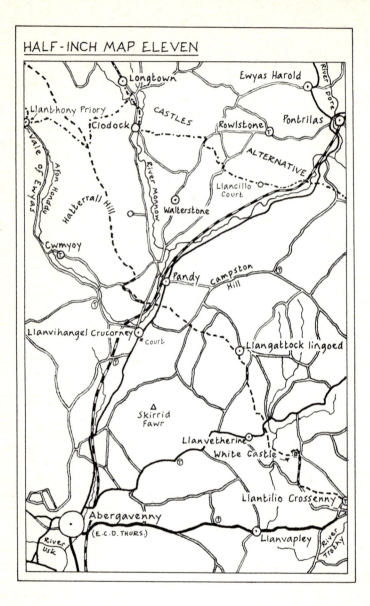

162

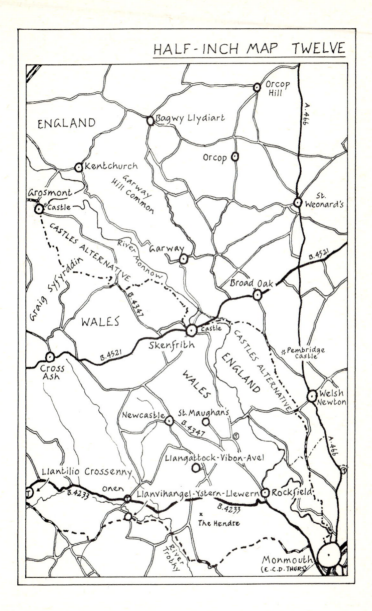

Church of St. Martin
Cwmyoy

This fascinating ancient church has withstood many centuries of gradual landslipping, little is left at rightangles. The Tower tilts alarmingly - hence the supporting flying buttresses.

All credit to its original builders whose work has stood such a tremendous test of durability.

THE CASTLE TO TRE-FEDW

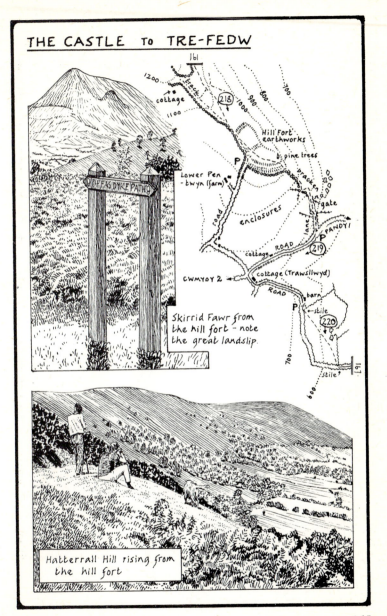

OFFAS DYKE PATH

Skirrid Fawr from
the hill fort – note
the great landslip.

Hatterrall Hill rising from
the hill fort

161

1200
cottage
1100
black...
218
1000
900
800
700
Hill Fort
earthworks
& pine trees
P
Lower Pen
-twyn (farm)
road
bracken
gate
enclosures
lane
PANDY1
P
219
cottage
ROAD
cottage (Trawsllwyd)
CWMYOY 2
ROAD
barn
P
stile
220
700
stile
191
600

Ysgyryd Fawr (Skirrid)

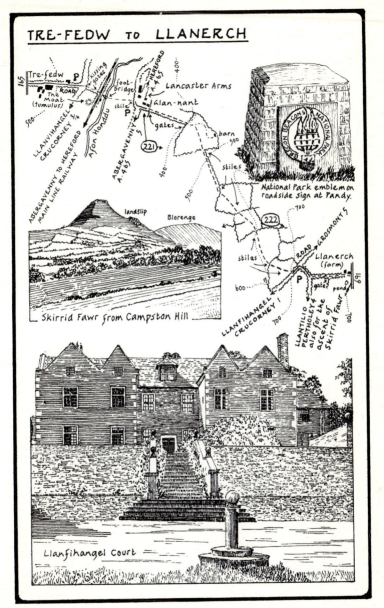

TRE-FEDW to LLANERCH

Tre-fedw

ABERGAVENNY TO HEREFORD MAIN LINE RAILWAY

The Moat (tumulus)

LLANVIHANGEL CRUCORNEY ¾

Afon Honddu

ABERGAVENNY A.465

missing gates

footbridge

stile

A.465 TO HEREFORD

Lancaster Arms

Glan-nant

gates

221

barn

stiles

National Park emblem on roadside sign at Pandy.

222

700

ROAD to GROSMONT 5

Llanerch (farm)

stiles

gates

pond

LLANFIHANGEL CRUCORNEY 1

LLANTILIO PERTHOLEY 4 also for the ascent of Skirrid Fawr

landslip

Blorenge

Skirrid Fawr from Campston Hill

Llanfihangel Court

167

St. Cadoc's Church at Llangattock Lingoed

The route enters Llangattock through the Old Primary School yard (this building is under consideration as a possible new Youth Hostel) and leaves via the church -yard path and down a pasture field into the valley of Full Brook. The village itself, though small, does possess a Post Office and a pub with an unusual name 'The Hunter's Moon'.

Old Court Farm

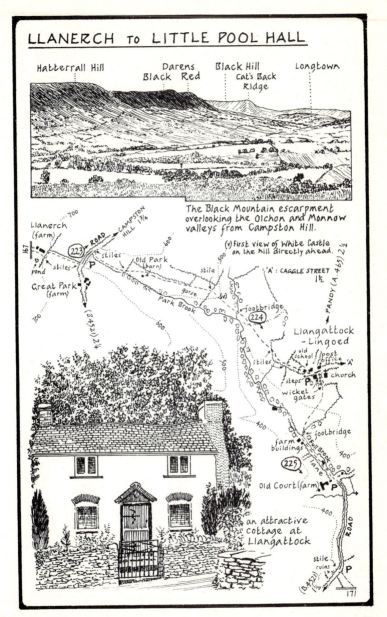

LLANERCH to LITTLE POOL HALL

The Black Mountain escarpment overlooking the Olchon and Monnow valleys from Campston Hill.

Hatterrall Hill

Darens
Black Red

Black Hill
Cat's Back
Ridge

Longtown

700

Llanerch
(farm)

CAMPSTON HILL 1¾

ROAD

223

stiles

D
pond

167

stiles

P

Great Park
(farm)

700

(B 4521) 2¼

Old Park
(barn)

600

gorse

Park Brook

600

(w)

500

(v) First view of White Castle
on the hill directly ahead.

stile

500

'A' : CAGGLE STREET
1½

footbridge

224

PANDY (A 465) 2½

Llangattock
- Lingoed

old
school
post
office

stiles

'A'

steps

P

church

wicket
gates

400

footbridge

500

farm
buildings

Full Brook

lane

225

400

Old Court (farm)

P

400

an attractive
cottage at
Llangattock

stile
ruins

(B 4521) ¼

P

ROAD

171

169

White Castle

LITTLE POOL HALL TO WHITE CASTLE

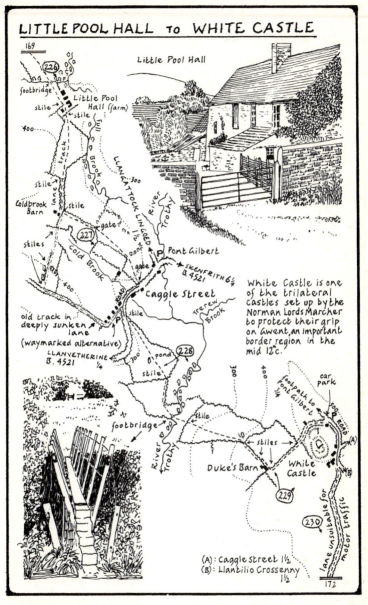

Little Pool Hall

169

226

footbridge
stile
Little Pool Hall (farm)
stile
stile
400

LLANGATTOCK LINGOED

Os Brook

River Trothy

300

Coldbrook Barn
stile
stile
227
Cold Brook
gate
400
gate

stiles
400

P Pont Gilbert
SKENFRITH 6¼ B.4521
Caggle Street
stile
ROAD
Trerew Brook

old track in deeply sunken lane
(waymarked alternative)
P

LLANVETHERINE B.4521 ¼
300
pond
228
stile

White Castle is one of the trilateral castles set up by the Norman Lords Marcher to protect their grip on Gwent, an important border region in the mid 12°C.

300
400
car park

footbridge

footpath to Pont Gilbert ¾
road

stile
stiles
White Castle
River & Trothy
Duke's Barn
229

230

lane unsuitable for motor traffic

(A): Caggle Street 1½
(B): Llantilio Crossenny 1½

172

171

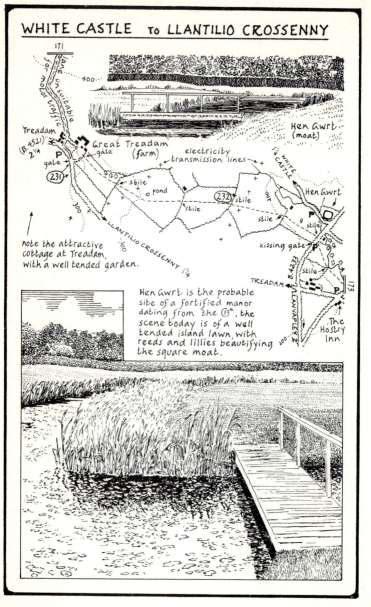

WHITE CASTLE TO LLANTILIO CROSSENNY

171

400

lane unsuitable for motor traffic

Treadam
(B 4521)
2¼

P

gate

231

gate

Great Treadam
(farm)

gate

sbile

electricity
transmission lines

300

o pond

500

232

stile

stile

stile

stile

Hen Gwrt
(moat)

WHITE CASTLE ¼

200

Hen Gwrt

P

stile

LLANTILIO CROSSENNY 1½

300

kissing gate

P

stile

B 4233

TREADAM

LLANVAPLEY 2

173

P

300

The
Hostry
Inn

note the attractive
cottage at Treadam,
with a well tended garden.

Hen Gwrt is the probable
site of a fortified manor
dating from the (13)th, the
scene today is of a well
tended island lawn, with
reeds and lillies beautifying
the square moat.

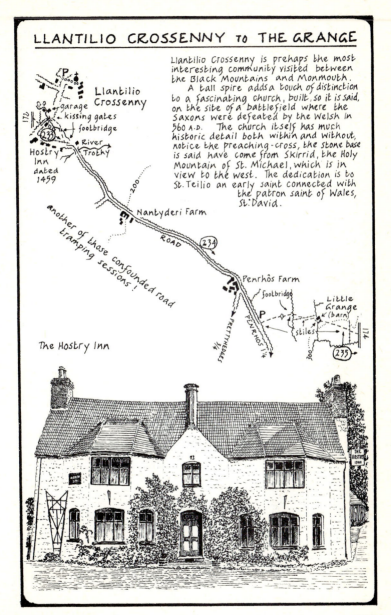

LLANTILIO CROSSENNY to THE GRANGE

Llantilio Crossenny is prehaps the most interesting community visited between the Black Mountains and Monmouth.

A tall spire adds a touch of distinction to a fascinating church, built, so it is said, on the site of a battlefield where the Saxons were defeated by the Welsh in 560 A.D. The church itself has much historic detail both within and without, notice the preaching-cross, the stone base is said have come from Skirrid, the Holy Mountain of St. Michael, which is in view to the west. The dedication is to St. Teilio an early saint connected with the patron saint of Wales, St. David.

P

Llantilio Crossenny

garage
kissing gates
footbridge

172

233

River Trothy

Hostry Inn dated 1459

200

another of these confounded road tramping sessions!

Nantyderi Farm

ROAD

234

Penrhôs Farm

footbridge

PRETTYHEDGES ¾

PENRHÔS ¼

P

stiles

Little Grange (barn)

300

235

174

The Hostry Inn

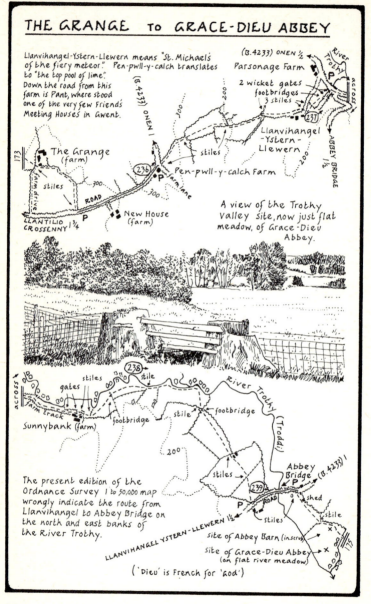

THE GRANGE TO GRACE-DIEU ABBEY

Llanvihangel-Ystern-Llewern means "St. Michael's of the fiery meteor." Pen-pwll-y-calch translates to "the top pool of lime." Down the road from this farm is Pant, where stood one of the very few Friends' Meeting Houses in Gwent.

(B.4233) ONEN ½
Parsonage Farm

River Trothy across

ONEN 1 (B.4233)

2 wicket gates
footbridges
3 stiles

237

The Grange (farm)

173

farm drive

stiles

300

ROAD

236

P

Farm lane

stiles

Pen-pwll-y-calch Farm

Llanvihangel -Ystern- Llewern

ABBEY BRIDGE 1½

200

300

P

New House (farm)

LLANTILIO CROSSENNY 1¾

A view of the Trothy Valley site, now just flat meadow, of Grace-Dieu Abbey.

238

tile

gates   stiles

stiles

River Trothy ('Trodd')

across

farm track

footbridge

stile

footbridge

Sunnybank (farm)

200

The present edition of the Ordnance Survey 1 to 50,000 map wrongly indicate the route from Llanvihangel to Abbey Bridge on the north and east banks of the River Trothy.

stiles

Abbey Bridge (B.4233)

P

239

P

ROAD

shed

stile

LLANVIHANGEL YSTERN-LLEWERN 1½

stiles

site of Abbey Barn (inscr)

site of Grace-Dieu Abbey (on flat river meadow)

175

('Dieu' is French for 'God')

GRACE-DIEU ABBEY TO WATERY LANE

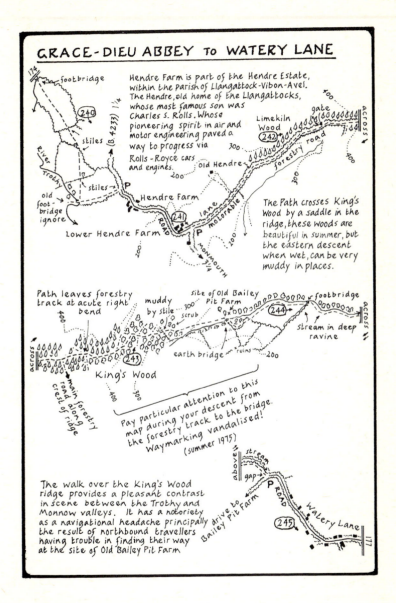

footbridge

240

stiles

(B.4233) 1¼

River Trothy

old footbridge ignore

stiles

P

Hendre Farm

241

ROAD

lane motorable

P

Lower Hendre Farm

200

MONMOUTH 3/4

Hendre Farm is part of the Hendre Estate, within the parish of Llangattock-Vibon-Avel. The Hendre, old home of the Llangattocks, whose most famous son was Charles S. Rolls. Whose pioneering spirit in air and motor engineering paved a way to progress via Rolls-Royce cars and engines.

old Hendre

200

300

Limekiln Wood

242

gate

across ¾

forestry road

400

300

400

The Path crosses King's Wood by a saddle in the ridge, these woods are beautiful in summer, but the eastern descent when wet, can be very muddy in places.

Path leaves forestry track at acute right bend

400

muddy by stile

300

scrub

site of Old Bailey Pit Farm

footbridge

244

across

stream in deep ravine

across

243

earth bridge

ruins

200

King's Wood

400

300

main forestry road along crest of ridge

Pay particular attention to this map during your descent from the forestry track to the bridge. Waymarking vandalised!
(summer 1975)

above

stream

gap

P

ROAD

drive to Bailey Pit Farm

245

Watery Lane

177

The walk over the King's Wood ridge provides a pleasant contrast in scene between the Trothy and Monnow valleys. It has a notoriety as a navigational headache principally the result of northbound travellers having trouble in finding their way at the site of Old Bailey Pit Farm

Monnow Bridge

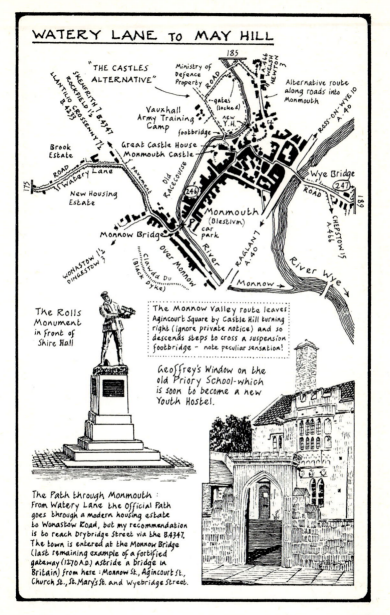

WATERY LANE TO MAY HILL

"THE CASTLES ALTERNATIVE"

SKENFRITH 7 B.4521
ROCKFIELD 1½ B.4347
LLANTILIO CROSSENNY 7½
B.4233

Ministry of Defence Property

185

B.466 WELSH NEWTON 3

Alternative route along roads into Monmouth

ROSS-ON-WYE 10 A.40

Vauxhall Army Training Camp

gates (locked)

new Y.H.

footbridge

Brook Estate

ROAD 175

Watery Lane

New Housing Estate

Great Castle House — Monmouth Castle —

pavement

OLD RACECOURSE

246

Monmouth (Blestivm)

car park

P

Wye Bridge

247

ROAD

189

CHEPSTOW 15 A.466

Monnow Bridge

over Monnow River

RAGLAN 7 A.40

WONASTOW 1½ DINGESTOW 3

Clawdd Du (BLACK DYKE)

Monnow

River Wye

The Rolls Monument in front of Shire Hall

The Monnow Valley route leaves Agincourt Square by Castle Hill turning right (ignore private notice) and so descends steps to cross a suspension footbridge – note peculiar sensation!

Geoffrey's Window on the old Priory School-which is soon to become a new Youth Hostel.

The Path through Monmouth:
From Watery Lane the Official Path goes through a modern housing estate to Wonastow Road, but my recommendation is to reach Drybridge Street via the B.4347. The town is entered at the Monnow Bridge (last remaining example of a fortified gateway (1270 A.D.) astride a bridge in Britain) from here: Monnow St., Agincourt St., Church St., St. Mary's St. and Wyebridge Street.

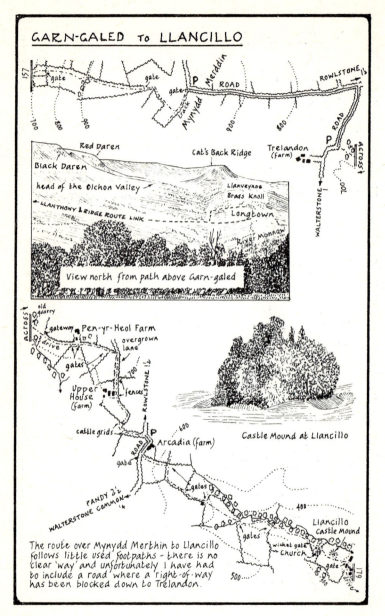

GARN-GALED to LLANCILLO

157

gate   gate   gate   P   Mynydd Meridin   ROAD   ROWLSTONE 1½

track   P   ACROSS

700   800   900   900   800

Red Daren   Cat's Back Ridge   Trelandon (farm)   ACROSS

Black Daren   Llanveynoe   Brass Knoll

head of the Olchon Valley   Longtown

LLANTHONY & RIDGE ROUTE LINK   River Monnow   WALTERSTONE 1   700

View north from path above Garn-galed

old quarry   ACROSS

gateway   Pen-yr-Heol Farm   overgrown lane

drive

gates   ROWLSTONE 1½

Upper House (farm)   fences

cattle grids   600

P   ROAD   Arcadia (farm)   Castle Mound at Llancillo

gate   gates

PANDY 2½   Llancillo

WALTERSTONE COMMON   gates   Castle Mound

wicket gate   Church   400

The route over Mynydd Merthin to Llancillo   500   gate   179
follows little used footpaths - there is no
clear 'way' and unfortunately I have had
to include a road where a right-of-way
has been blocked down to Trelandon.

178

LLANCILLO TO GROSMONT

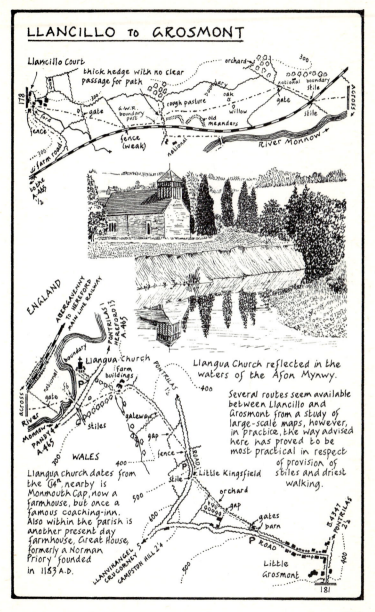

Llancillo Court

thick hedge with no clear passage for path

orchard   300
boundary
national boundary stile
oak
willow   gate
stile   Across
A.W.R. boundary post
rough pasture
gate   old meanders
178
ford   fence
national
fence (weak)
to the A.465   farm road   River Monnow
300

Llangua Church reflected in the waters of the Afon Mynwy.

ENGLAND

ABERGAVENNY TO HEREFORD MAIN LINE RAILWAY
PONTRILAS HEREFORD 13 A.465
boundary
national
Llangua Church
farm buildings
P
Across
River
gate
Monnow PANDY 4 A.465
stiles
gateway
gap
fence
WALES
400
PONTRILAS 1½
400
ROAD

Several routes seem available between Llancillo and Grosmont from a study of large-scale maps, however, in practice, the way advised here has proved to be most practical in respect of provision of stiles and driest walking.

Llangua church dates from the 14th, nearby is Monmouth Cap, now a farmhouse, but once a famous coaching-inn. Also within the parish is another present day farmhouse, Great House, formerly a Norman Priory founded in 1153 A.D.

P
stile   Little Kingsfield
500
orchard
gap
600
gates   barn
ROAD   B4347 PONTRILAS 2½
500
P ROAD
LLANVIHANGEL CRUCORNEY 5 CAMPSTON HILL 2¼
Little Grosmont
400
181

179

Grosmont Castle

GROSMONT TO GRAIG SYFYRDDIN

The village of Grosmont was a medieval town with a far larger population than it possesses today. The village is built on a hill above the meandering Monnow, facing Graig Syfyrdin.

Grosmont has numerous appealing faces, including a Market Hall built in 1832. The church is not merely large, but its great bulk possesses a rare elegance that must surely gain it many admirers, it is in truth an inspired piece of ecclesiastical construction. Grosmont Castle, which stands shyly back out of sight of the casual visitor, who may pass through unaware of its presence, is the first of the Trilateral group encountered on this alternative. It runs a close second to White Castle, which possesses a watered moat, however, here there is much to see and marvel upon, including a highly ornate C14th chimney which stands while all about it has fallen.

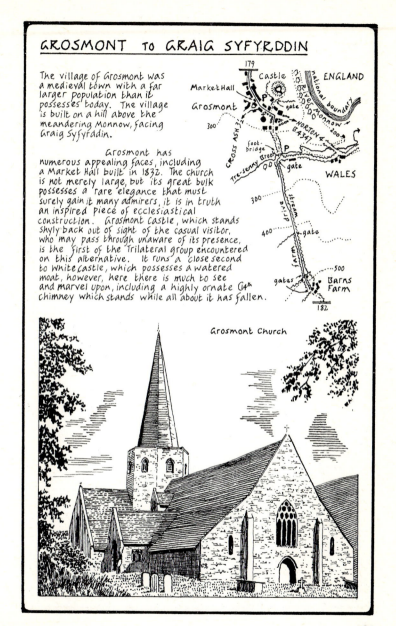

Grosmont Church

GRAIG SYFYRDDIN to SKENFRITH

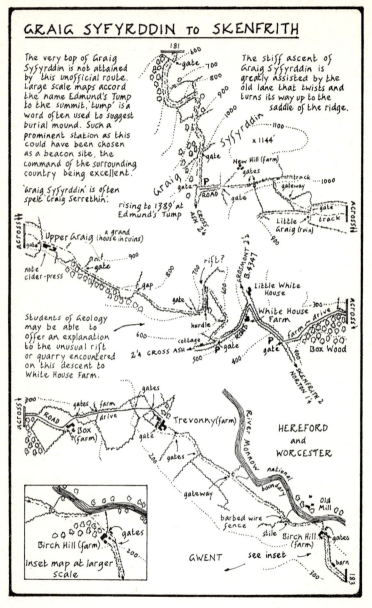

The very top of Graig Syfyrddin is not attained by this unofficial route. Large scale maps accord the name Edmund's Tump to the summit, 'tump' is a word often used to suggest burial mound. Such a prominent station as this could have been chosen as a beacon site, the command of the surrounding country being excellent.

'Graig Syfyrddin' is often spelt 'Craig Serrethin'.

rising to 1389' at Edmund's Tump

The stiff ascent of Graig Syfyrddin is greatly assisted by the old lane that twists and turns its way up to the saddle of the ridge.

Students of Geology may be able to offer an explanation to the unusual rift or quarry encountered on this descent to White House Farm.

181
600
gate 700
800
900
1000

Syfyrddin
x 1144' 1100
New Hill (farm)
gates track
gateway 1000

Graig
gate P
ROAD gate
gate
Little Graig (ruin)
track
ACROSS↓

Upper Graig
a grand (house in ruins)
gate
note cider-press
rift gate
gap
900
800
rift?
gate
600
cottage
2¼ CROSS ASH 500
ROCHMONT 2¼ B.4347
Little White House
White House Farm
hurdle
P gate
P gate
400
farm drive
Box Wood
SKENFRITH 2 NORTON 1¼
ACROSS↑

300
gates farm drive
ACROSS↓ ROAD
Box (farm)
200
gates
gates
gate
Trevonny (farm)
gateway
River Monnow
national boundary
barbed wire fence
stile
Birch Hill (farm)
see inset
Old Mill
gates
barn
183

HEREFORD and WORCESTER

GWENT

Birch Hill (farm)
gates
200
Inset map at larger scale

SKENFRITH TO PEMBRIDGE CASTLE

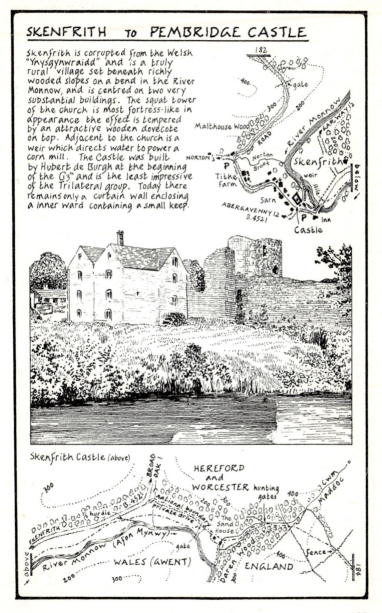

Skenfrith is corrupted from the Welsh "Ynysgynwraidd" and is a truly rural village set beneath richly wooded slopes on a bend in the River Monnow, and is centred on two very substantial buildings. The squat tower of the church is most fortress-like in appearance the effect is tempered by an attractive wooden dovecote on top. Adjacent to the church is a weir which directs water to power a corn mill. The Castle was built by Hubert de Burgh at the beginning of the C3" and is the least impressive of the Trilateral group. Today there remains only a curtain wall enclosing a inner ward containing a small keep.

Skenfrith Castle (above)

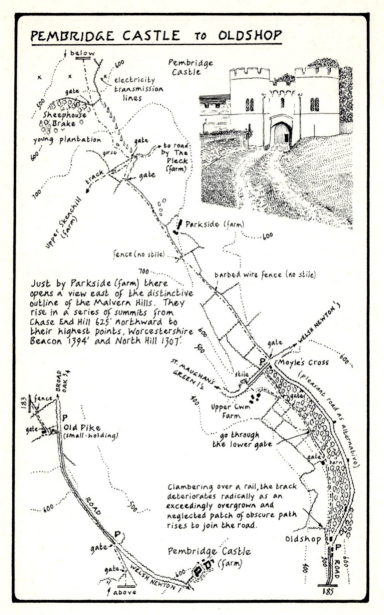

PEMBRIDGE CASTLE TO OLDSHOP

to below

electricity
transmission
lines

Pembridge
Castle

600

gate

500

Sheephouse
Brake

young plantation

600

gate

gorse

to road
by The
Pleck
(farm)

gate

track

700

Upper Skenchill
(farm)

Parkside (farm)

600

fence (no stile)

700

barbed wire fence (no stile)

Just by Parkside (farm) there
opens a view east of the distinctive
outline of the Malvern Hills. They
rise in a series of summits from
Chase End Hill 625' northward to
their highest points, Worcestershire
Beacon 1394' and North Hill 1307'.

WELSH NEWTON

gate

600

ST. MAUGHAN'S
GREEN 1½

600

500

P

Moyle's Cross

stile

(pleasant road as alternative)

400

Upper Cwm
Farm

gate

BROAD
OAK ¾

183

fence

go through
the lower gate

gate
barn

gate

P

Old Pike
(small-holding)

ROAD

600

500

Clambering over a rail, the track
deteriorates radically as an
exceedingly overgrown and
neglected patch of obscure path
rises to join the road.

Oldshop

P

400   500

ROAD

600

P

gate

Pembridge Castle
(farm)

gate

WELSH NEWTON

600

P D

above

185

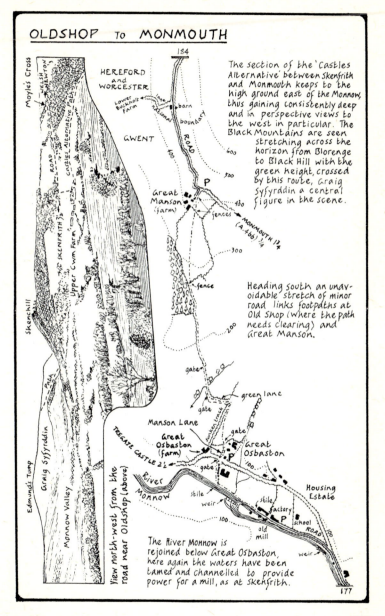

OLDSHOP TO MONMOUTH

184

HEREFORD and WORCESTER

GWENT

Moyle's Cross

WELSH NEWTON 3½

Lower Bucknolt Farm

barn

NATIONAL BOUNDARY

ROAD

600

500

400

P

Great Manson (farm)

430

fences

MONMOUTH 1½ (A.466) ¾

300

fence

200

Skenhill

CASTLES ALTERNATIVE PATH

TO SKENFRITH 3½

Upper Cwm Farm

ROAD

gate

gate

green lane

Manson Lane

Great Osbaston (farm)

gate

P

Great Osbaston

TREGATE CASTLE 2½

gate

Path

Edmund's Tump

Graig Syfyrddin

Monnow Valley

View north-west from the road near Oldshop (above)

River Monnow

stile

weir

100

old mill

stile

P

factory

school

Housing Estate

ROAD

weir

The section of the 'Castles Alternative' between Skenfrith and Monmouth keeps to the high ground east of the Monnow, thus gaining consistently deep and in perspective views to the west in particular. The Black Mountains are seen stretching across the horizon from Blorenge to Black Hill with the green height, crossed by this route, Graig Syfyrddin a central figure in the scene.

Heading south an unavoidable stretch of minor road links footpaths at Old Shop (where the path needs clearing) and Great Manson.

The River Monnow is rejoined below Great Osbaston, here again the waters have been tamed and channelled to provide power for a mill, as at Skenfrith.

177

185

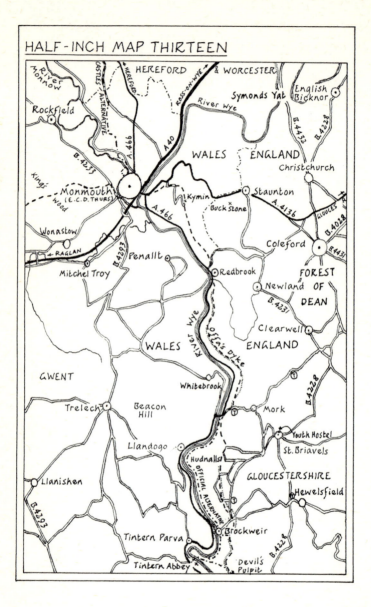

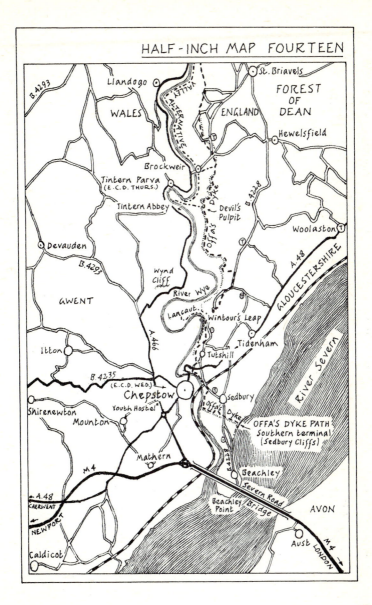

187

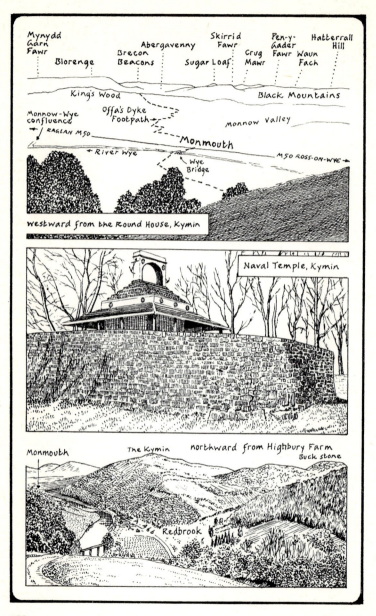

Mynydd Garn Fawr

Blorenge

Brecon Beacons

Abergavenny

Sugar Loaf

Skirrid Fawr

Crug Mawr

Pen-y-Gader Fawr

Waun Fach

Hatterrall Hill

King's Wood

Black Mountains

Monnow-Wye confluence

Offa's Dyke Footpath

Monnow Valley

RAGLAN M50

Monmouth

← River Wye

M50 ROSS-ON-WYE →

Wye Bridge

westward from the Round House, Kymin

Naval Temple, Kymin

Monmouth

The Kymin

northward from Highbury Farm

Buck Stone

Redbrook

MAY HILL to HIGHBURY FARM

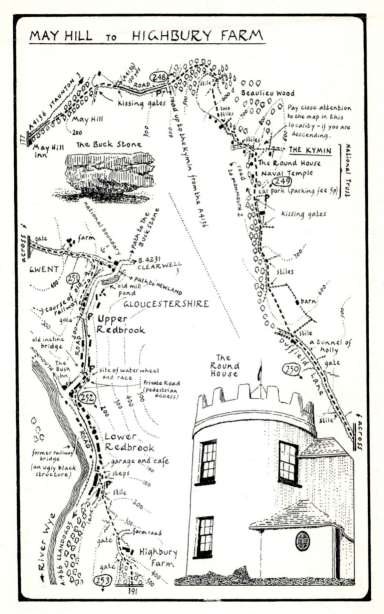

A4136 STAUNTON 2

(A4136) ROAD

248

kissing gates

May Hill

The Buck Stone

177

200

May Hill Inn

300

road up to the Kymin from the A4136

400

stile

Beaulieu Wood

two stiles

stiles

Pay close attention to the map in this locality — if you are descending.

THE KYMIN

The Round House

Naval Temple

249

car park (parking fee 5p)

kissing gates

National Trust

road to Monmouth 2

national boundary

Path to The Buck Stone

gate

farm

GWENT

251

B.4231 CLEARWELL 3

Path to NEWLAND

old mill pond

GLOUCESTERSHIRE

course of old railway

gate

Upper Redbrook

old incline bridge

MONMOUTH 2

The Bush Inn

site of waterwheel and race

252

Private Road (pedestrian access)

stiles

barn

stile

a tunnel of holly

gate

Duffield Lane

250

stile

across

The Round House

ROAD

Lower Redbrook

garage and cafe

steps

stile

former railway bridge (an ugly black structure)

100

100

200

River Wye

A466 LLANDOGO 5

farm road

gate

gate

Highbury Farm

253

191

Offa's Dyke in Creeping Hill Wood

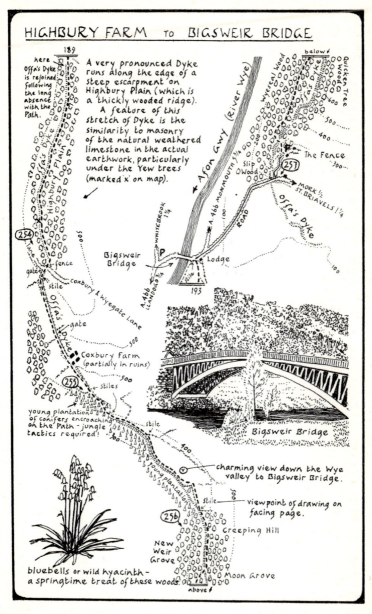

HIGHBURY FARM to BIGSWEIR BRIDGE

here Offa's Dyke is rejoined following the long absence with the Path.

A very pronounced Dyke runs along the edge of a steep escarpment on Highbury Plain (which is a thickly wooded ridge).

A feature of this stretch of Dyke is the similarity to masonry of the natural weathered limestone in the actual earthwork, particularly under the Yew trees (marked 'x' on map).

Afon Gwy (River Wye)

189

Highbury Plain

254

gate fence

stile

Coxbury & Wyegate Lane

gate 500

Coxbury Farm (partially in ruins)

255

stiles 500

young plantation of conifers encroaching on the Path — jungle tactics required!

stile

A.466 MONMOUTH 3½

A.466 LLANDOGO ¼

WHITEBROOK 1¼

P

Bigsweir Bridge

Lodge

193

Wyereal Wood

below

Quicken Tree Wood

600

500

400

Slip Wood

The Fence

251

MORK ½
ST. BRIAVELS 1¼

Offa's Dyke

300

100

charming view down the Wye valley to Bigsweir Bridge.

viewpoint of drawing on facing page.

stile 500

256

Creeping Hill

New Weir Grove

Moon Grove

above

bluebells or wild hyacinth – a springtime treat of these woods.

Bigsweir Bridge

191

St. Briavel's Castle

St. Briavel's Castle may be espied from Offa's Dyke Path down at Bigsweir Bridge, for it holds a commanding position high above the swiftly flowing, tidal Wye - which normally ceases to be tidal at this point. It is also very much a part of the Royal Forest of Dean, over which the Castle's role was administrative and judicial. It certainly existed back in the early C2th and has subsequently been used as a Royal Hunting Lodge during medieval times, an arsenal when iron weaponry was produced in the Forest and most recently as a Youth Hostel. The drawing here is of the great Gatehouse, the principal feature of a Castle that never stood as an impregnable fortress. Today it may be enjoyed by anyone for the moat - which is dry - is like a garden and the views are very extensive, with Skirrid Fawr drawing the eye westward toward the Black Mountains. Below the Castle is an embayment occupied now by the feeding streams of Mork Brook, this was once filled by the Wye, it being an abandoned meander.

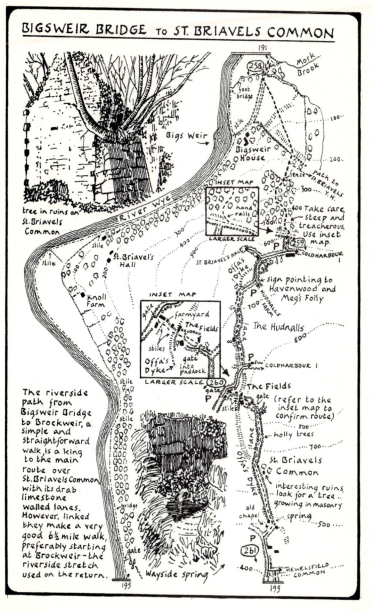

BIGSWEIR BRIDGE TO ST. BRIAVELS COMMON

191

Mork Brook

258

foot bridge

stile

Bigs Weir

Bigsweir House

tree in ruins on St. Briavels Common

River Wye

100

200

300

fence

path to ST. BRIAVELS Y.H.

INSET MAP

hand rails

LARGER SCALE

400 Take care, steep and treacherous. Use inset map.

stile

St. Briavel's Hall

100

200

300

ST. BRIAVEL'S HALL

400

500

600

P 259

COLDHARBOUR

Knoll Farm

Offa's Dyke

sign pointing to Havenwood and Meg's Folly

INSET MAP

gate

farmyard

The Fields

stiles

Offa's Dyke

gate into paddock

LARGER SCALE

P 260

HUDNALLS FARM

700

The Hudnalls

800

P

COLDHARBOUR 1

stile

The riverside path from Bigsweir Bridge to Brockweir, a simple and straightforward walk is a king to the main route over St. Briavels Common with its drab limestone walled lanes. However, linked they make a very good 6½ mile walk, preferably starting at Brockweir - the riverside stretch used on the return.

stile

stile

stile

stile

bridge

gate

gate

The Fields

gate (refer to the inset map to confirm route)

stiles

800

holly trees

700

St. Briavels Common

interesting ruins, look for a tree growing in masonry

old chapel

spring

500

P 261

400

HEWELSFIELD COMMON

195

Wayside spring

195

Tintern Abbey

194

ST. BRIAVELS COMMON to SHORN CLIFF

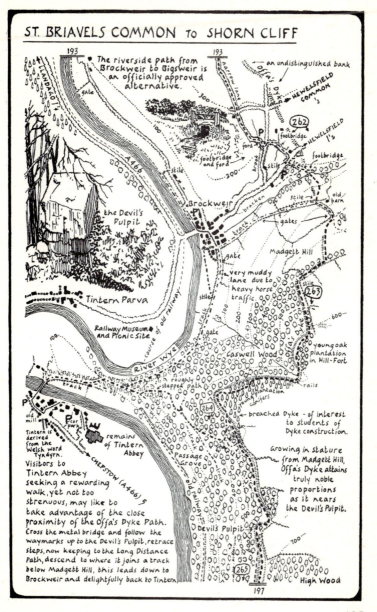

The riverside path from Brockweir to Bigsweir is an officially approved alternative.

193   193

an undistinguished bank

LLANDOGO

HEWELSFIELD COMMON

gate

262

foorbridge

HEWELSFIELD 1½

P

ford

foorbridge

narrow lane

Offa's Dyke

A466

stile

300

100

200

footbridge and ford

stile

stile   old barn

Brockweir

bracken

gates

100

track

Madgett Hill

gate

very muddy lane due to heavy horse traffic

263

stile

the Devil's Pulpit

stiles

200

600

Tintern Parva

Railway Museum and Picnic Site

course of old railway

gate

Caswell Wood

young oak plantation in Hill-Fort

River Wye

roughly stepped path

264

rails

P

Track

old mill

Car park

wood plantation conifers

breached Dyke - of interest to students of Dyke construction.

Tintern is derived from the Welsh word Tyndyrn.

remains of Tintern Abbey

CHEPSTOW (A466) 5

Passage Grove

Growing in stature from Madgett Hill, Offa's Dyke attains truly noble proportions as it nears the Devil's Pulpit.

Visitors to Tintern Abbey seeking a rewarding walk, yet not too strenuous, may like to take advantage of the close proximity of the Offa's Dyke Path. Cross the metal bridge and follow the waymarks up to the Devil's Pulpit, retrace steps, now keeping to the Long Distance Path, descend to where it joins a track below Madgett Hill, this leads down to Brockweir and delightfully back to Tintern

Devil's Pulpit

700

265

High Wood

197

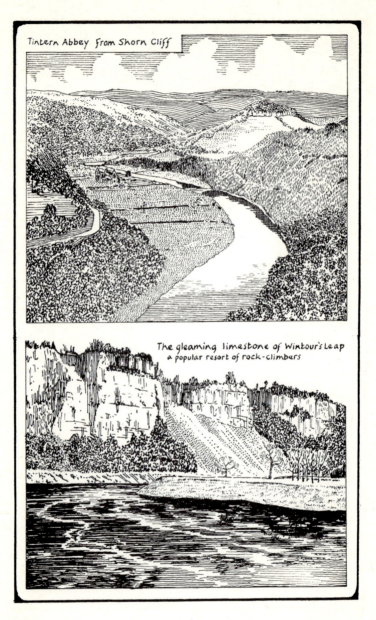

Tintern Abbey from Shorn Cliff

The gleaming limestone of Wintour's Leap
a popular resort of rock-climbers

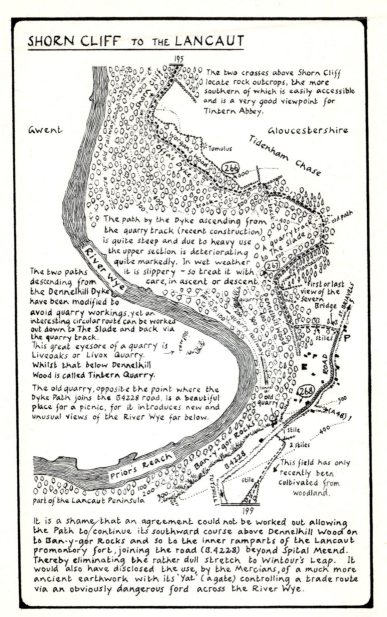

SHORN CLIFF TO THE LANCAUT

195

The two crosses above Shorn Cliff locate rock outcrops, the more southern of which is easily accessible and is a very good viewpoint for Tintern Abbey.

Gwent

Gloucestershire

Tidenham Chase

Shorn Cliff

course old railway

Offa's Dyke

Horsan's Wood

Tumulus

266

600

track

Tumulus

The path by the Dyke ascending from the quarry track (recent construction) is quite steep and due to heavy use the upper section is deteriorating quite markedly. In wet weather it is slippery ~ so treat it with care, in ascent or descent.

old path

A quarry track to The Slade

267

plantation

The two paths descending from the Dennelhill Dyke have been modified to avoid quarry workings, yet an interesting circular route can be worked out down to The Slade and back via the quarry track.

This great eyesore of a quarry is Liveoaks or Livox Quarry. Whilst that below Dennelhill Wood is called Tintern Quarry.

The old quarry, opposite the point where the Dyke Path joins the B4228 road, is a beautiful place for a picnic, for it introduces new and unusual views of the River Wye far below.

River Wye

quarry

quarry railway

first or last view of the Severn Bridge

ST. BRIAVELS

stiles

P

E

ROAD

tunnel

old quarry

268

500

(A48)

old quarry

tunnel

Ban-y-gor Rocks

B4228

stile

2 stiles

1 stile

400

This field has only recently been cultivated from woodland.

Priors Reach

100 200 300

part of the Lancaut Peninsula

TUTSHILL

199

It is a shame that an agreement could not be worked out allowing the Path to continue its southward course above Dennelhill Wood on to Ban-y-gor Rocks and so to the inner ramparts of the Lancaut promontory fort, joining the road (B.4228) beyond Spital Meend. Thereby eliminating the rather dull stretch to Wintour's Leap. It would also have disclosed the use, by the Mercians, of a much more ancient earthwork with its 'Yat' (a gate) controlling a trade route via an obviously dangerous ford across the River Wye.

197

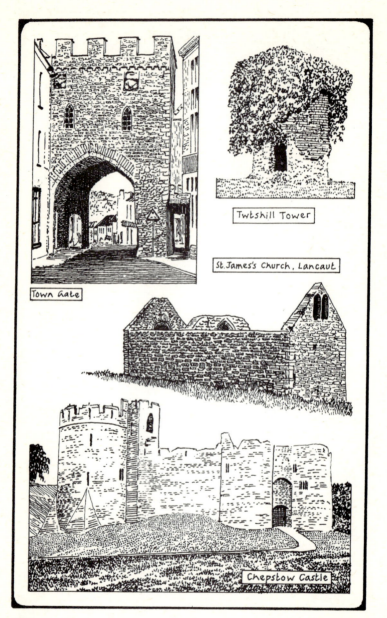

Town Gate

Twtshill Tower

St. James's Church, Lancaut

Chepstow Castle

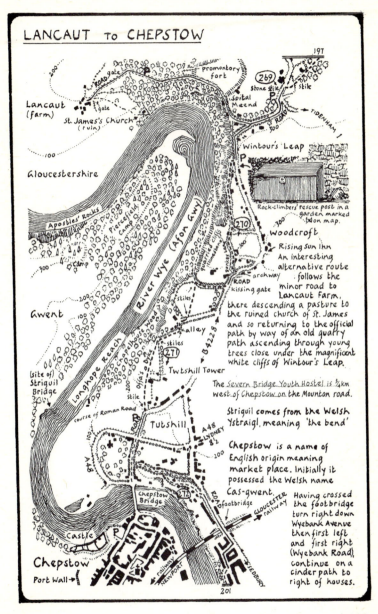

Offa's Dyke at
Pennsylvania Village
- Mercian Way

With the Sedbury Cliff
skyline in view, this
great Dark Age earthwork,
here so sadly neglected
and overgrown, makes
one final show of strength,
as it slices off the Beachley
peninsula from what was
the south-western limit
of King Offa's Mercian
kingdom.   This bold
piece of frontiersmanship
surely here deserves
better recognition,
could not a plaque be
placed on Offa's Tump
briefly recounting the
history of Offa's Dyke?

What is the SLIMEROAD?
The Slimeroad was used by
in coming ships, if they
missed the tide, grounding
here for safety.

CHEPSTOW TO SEDBURY CLIFFS

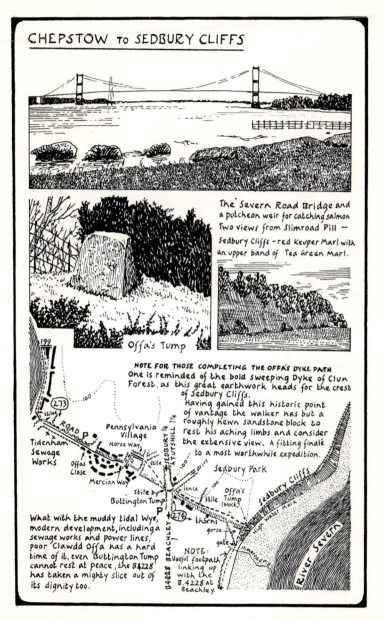

The Severn Road Bridge and a putcheon weir for catching salmon. Two views from Slimroad Pill —

Sedbury Cliffs - red Keuper Marl with an upper band of Tea Green Marl.

Offa's Tump

NOTE FOR THOSE COMPLETING THE OFFA'S DYKE PATH
One is reminded of the bold sweeping Dyke of Clun Forest, as this great earthwork heads for the crest of Sedbury Cliffs.

Having gained this historic point of vantage the walker has but a roughly hewn sandstone block to rest his aching limbs and consider the extensive view. A fitting finale to a most worthwhile expedition.

Tidenham Sewage Works

Pennsylvania Village

Norse Way

Offa's Close

Mercian Way

stile by Buttington Tump

Sedbury Park

Offa's Tump (block)

stile

fence

drive

thorns

gorse

gate

Sedbury Cliffs

High Water Mark

River Severn

Slimroad Pill

NOTE: Useful footpath linking up with the B.4228 at Beachley.

What with the muddy tidal Wye, modern development, including a sewage works and power lines, poor Clawdd Offa has a hard time of it, even Buttington Tump cannot rest at peace, the B4228 has taken a mighty slice out of its dignity too.

A PROFILE OF
OFFA'S DYKE PATH

Note symbol .... which indicates where Path and Offa's Dyke coincide

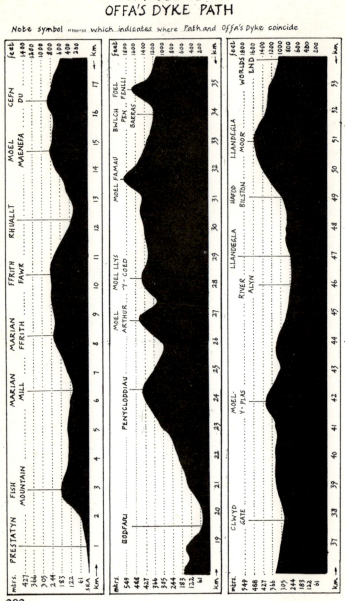

202

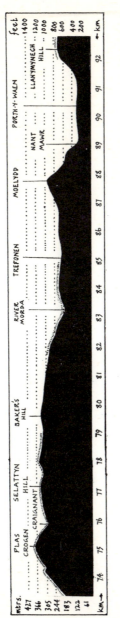

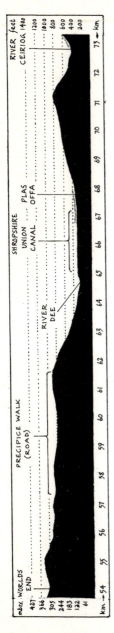

203

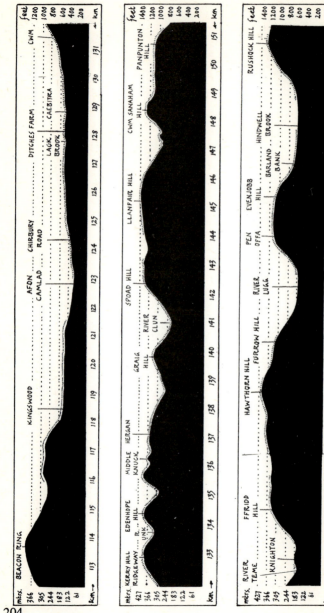

Top profile:

mtrs. — 366, 305, 244, 183, 122, 61
feet — 1200, 1000, 800, 600, 400, 200

BEACON RING ... KINGSWOOD ... AFON CAMLAD ... CHIRBURY ROAD ... DITCHES FARM ... LAGK BROOK ... CAEBITRA ... CWM

km → 113 114 115 116 117 118 119 120 121 122 123 124 125 126 127 128 129 130 131

Middle profile:

mtrs. — 427, 366, 305, 244, 183, 122, 61
feet — 1400, 1200, 1000, 800, 600, 400, 200

KERRY HILL ... RIDGEWAY ... R. UNK HILL ... EDENHOPE HILL ... MIDDLE KNUCK ... HERGAN ... CRAIG HILL ... RIVER CLUN ... SPOAD HILL ... LLANFAIR HILL ... CWM SANAHAM HILL ... PANPUNTON HILL

km → 133 134 135 136 137 138 139 140 141 142 143 144 145 146 147 148 149 150 151

Bottom profile:

mtrs. — 427, 366, 305, 244, 183, 122, 61
feet — 1400, 1200, 1000, 800, 600, 400, 200

RIVER TEME ... KNIGHTON ... FFRIDD HILL ... HAWTHORN HILL ... FURROW HILL ... RIVER LUGG ... PEN OFFA ... EVENJOBB HILL ... HINDWELL BROOK ... GARLAND BANK ... RUSHOCK HILL

km → 152 153 154 155 156 157 158 159 160 161 162 163 164 165 166 167 168 169 170

204

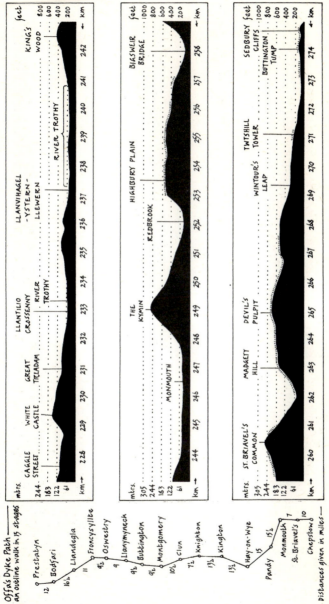

Offa's Dyke Path
an outline walk in 15 stages

Stage profiles (feet / km):

KING'S WOOD — CAGGLE STREET, WHITE CASTLE, GREAT TICLADAM, LLANTILIO CROSSENNY, RIVER TROTHY, LLANVIHAGEL-YSTERN-LLEWERN, RIVER TROTHY
(mtrs. 244, 183, 122, 61; km 228–242; feet 800, 600, 400, 200)

BIGSWEIR BRIDGE — MONMOUTH, THE KYMIN, REDBROOK, HIGHBURY PLAIN
(mtrs. 305, 244, 183, 122, 61; km 244–258; feet 1000, 800, 600, 400, 200)

SEDBURY CLIFFS — ST. BRIAVEL'S COMMON, MADGETT HILL, DEVIL'S PULPIT, WINTOUR'S LEAP, TWTSHILL TOWER, BUTTINGTON TUMP
(mtrs. 305, 244, 183, 122, 61; km 260–274; feet 1000, 800, 600, 400, 200)

Route map (distances given in miles):

Prestatyn 12
Bodfari
Llandegla 16½
11
Froncysyllte 9½
Oswestry 9
Llanymynech 9½
Buttington 9½
Montgomery 10½
Clun 7½
Knighton 13½
Kington 13½
Hay-on-Wye 15
Pandy 15½
Monmouth 7
St. Briavel's 10
Chepstow

Distances given in miles

205

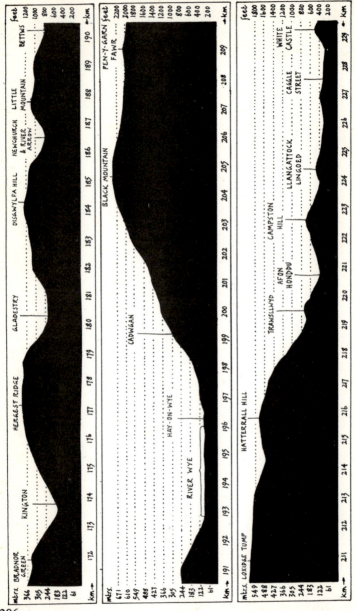

Top profile:

feet: 1200, 1000, 800, 600, 400, 200 → km

mtrs: 366, 305, 244, 183, 122, 61

BRADNOR GREEN · KINGTON · HERGEST RIDGE · GLADESTRY · DISGWYLFA HILL · NEWCHURCH & RIVER ARROW · LITTLE MOUNTAIN · BETTWS

km → 172 173 174 175 176 177 178 179 180 181 182 183 184 185 186 187 188 189 190

Middle profile:

feet: 2200, 2000, 1800, 1600, 1400, 1200, 1000, 800, 600, 400, 200 → km

mtrs: 671, 610, 549, 488, 427, 366, 305, 244, 183, 122, 61

RIVER WYE · HAY-ON-WYE · CADWGAN · BLACK MOUNTAIN · PEN-Y-GARN FAWR

km → 191 192 193 194 195 196 197 198 199 200 201 202 203 204 205 206 207 208 209

Bottom profile:

feet: 1800, 1600, 1400, 1200, 1000, 800, 600, 400, 200 → km

mtrs: 549, 488, 427, 366, 305, 244, 183, 122, 61

LOXIDAE TUMP · HATTERALL HILL · TRAWSLLWYD · AFON HONDDU · CAMPSTON HILL · LLANGATTOCK LINGOED · WHITE CASTLE · CAGGLE STREET · PEN-Y-GARN FAWR

km → 211 212 213 214 215 216 217 218 219 220 221 222 223 224 225 226 227 228 229

206

INDEX TO PLACE-NAMES

useful references from
large-scale maps only